BUILDING BRIDGES

Connecting Faculty, Students, and the College Library

MONTY L. McADOO

AMERICAN LIBRARY ASSOCIATION
CHICAGO   2010

Monty L. McAdoo is instructional services librarian of the Baron-Forness Library at Edinboro University of Pennsylvania in Edinboro, Pennsylvania. His research interests include faculty understanding and use of information literacy and information technology. He is also interested in the philosophy of library and information science. McAdoo earned his master's degree in library science at the University of Pittsburgh and his doctorate of education in administration and leadership studies at Indiana University of Pennsylvania.

The paper used in this publication meets the minimum requirements of American National Standard for Information Sciences—Permanence of Paper for Printed Library Materials, ANSI Z39.48-1992. ⊗

Library of Congress Cataloging-in-Publication Data
McAdoo, Monty L.
    Building bridges : connecting faculty, students, and the college library / Monty L. McAdoo.
        p. cm.
    Includes bibliographical references and index.
    ISBN 978-0-8389-1019-1 (alk. paper)
    1. Academic libraries—Relations with faculty and curriculum. 2. Information literacy—Study and teaching (Higher). 3. Library orientation for college students. 4. College teaching. 5. Libraries and students. I. Title.
    Z675.U5M358 2010
    027.7—dc22

                                                                    2009028889

ISBN-13: 978-0-8389-1019-1

Printed in the United States of America
14 13 12 11 10   5 4 3 2 1

To my bridge, Michelle, for all of her support,
patience, understanding, and more

CONTENTS

INTRODUCTION   vii

PART I   THE NEED FOR BRIDGES: CREATING
           A CONTEXT FOR SUCCESS

   ONE   Information Literacy and the Need for Effective Assignments   3

PART II   BUILDING A FOUNDATION: LIBRARIAN-
           FACULTY COLLABORATION

   TWO   Working with Faculty and the Curriculum   13

PART III   BUILDING THE BRIDGE: DEVELOPING
           EFFECTIVE LIBRARY ASSIGNMENTS

 THREE   Common Reasons Assignments Fail   33

  FOUR   Using Information Technology   45

  FIVE   Writing-from-Sources and Essay Assignments   55

   SIX   Term/Research Papers   67

 SEVEN   Citing Sources and Information Ethics   75

 EIGHT   Assignments in the Online Environment   83

PART IV   BRIDGE COLLAPSE! LIBRARY
           ASSIGNMENTS THAT FAIL

NINE   Tours   93

TEN   Scavenger Hunts   101

PART V   CROSSING THE BRIDGE: WORKING WITH
           FACULTY-DEVELOPED LIBRARY ASSIGNMENTS

ELEVEN   In the Classroom   117

TWELVE   In the Library   125

THIRTEEN   Some Final Words   133

APPENDIX A ASSOCIATION OF COLLEGE AND RESEARCH LIBRARIES
           INFORMATION LITERACY COMPETENCY STANDARDS
           FOR HIGHER EDUCATION   135

APPENDIX B DEFINING MOMENTS IN INFORMATION LITERACY   143

APPENDIX C OVERVIEW OF INSTRUCTION IN AMERICAN LIBRARIES   147

REFERENCES   151

INDEX   153

INTRODUCTION

ASSIGNMENTS ARE THE BRIDGES between the classroom and true learning.

This premise serves as the foundation for the entire book. Obviously, the size of the gap between a lack of understanding and understanding varies by student. When created and administered effectively, though, assignments allow students to successfully navigate and cross these gaps—regardless of the size of the gap. That is, assignments act as bridges between the content conveyed by the professor and both students' understanding of that content and their incorporation of it into their knowledge bases.

The need for effective assignments is perhaps best demonstrated by the consequences that can result from the administration of an ineffective assignment. Among the many consequences may be one or a combination of the following:

1. Lower grades

2. Increased anxiety over present or future assignments

3. Feelings of confusion, frustration, and self-doubt

4. Diminished quality of the final product

5. Failure to grasp the concepts being conveyed

6. Inability to master the content being conveyed

7. Lowered ability to successfully participate in an information-rich society

Ineffective assignments also have consequences for the faculty members who make them. Some of these include

1. Diminished reputation in the eyes of their peers and colleagues

2. Diminished reputation in the eyes of students, who may equate ineffective assignments with ineffective teaching or teachers

3. Frustration that students don't complete assignments as intended

4. Lowered expectations caused by the perceived inferiority of students' previously submitted work

5. Students' avoidance of future courses taught by such professors

6. Watering-down of assignments so that students get it

Because of the nature of their work, librarians are often bridges between the student and the faculty member. For example, working directly with students as they attempt to complete their assignments, librarians are likely to be the first to see the problems with assignments and to see firsthand how students actually navigate these problems and otherwise complete their work. In addition, librarians are typically perceived as neutral or on the same level as faculty members. As a result, students often approach and ask librarians to interpret assignments, to make suggestions, and, in some cases, to speak with a faculty member on their behalf to indicate that they tried but simply could not complete the assignment.

But librarians' roles should not start and stop on the front lines. Librarians can and should play a role in the development of assignments as well. Because we work with students on a daily basis, we see firsthand what works and what doesn't. Consequently, we can provide valuable insight into how to improve an assignment or otherwise modify it to help ensure it's achieving its intended objectives. Sometimes the glitches may be as simple as a typographical error that prevents students from locating a required source. Other times, the problems may be more involved or may revolve around the practical aspects of the assignment (e.g., students working in groups vs. independently)—problems and issues of which faculty members are often unaware or are unclear about how to resolve.

The idea of assignments and librarians serving as bridges is reflected in the organization of this book.

Part I: The Need for Bridges. This section provides a brief history and discussion of both information literacy and instruction in libraries. In so doing, it provides both evidence of and a rationale for the need to create effective assignments. The section concludes with a brief summary of some of the ways information literacy can play a role in that process.

Part II: Building a Foundation. Like any construction project, successful bridge building begins with a firm foundation. In terms of creating effective assignments, librarian–faculty-member collaboration serves as that foundation. This section provides a discussion of some of the many issues and concerns involving working and interacting with faculty members. Suggestions for improving librarian–faculty-member relationships and for taking a more active role with the curriculum are also provided.

Part III: Building the Bridge. With a firm foundation in place, the next step is actually building the bridge. To that end, each chapter in this section looks at a specific type of assignment involving the library. Among other things, definitions, a discussion of various assignment-specific issues, and examples of what can go wrong as well as suggestions about how to address problems are included for each type of assignment.

Part IV: Bridge Collapse! This section looks specifically at tours and scavenger hunts and discusses how and why they almost always fail when used as academic assignments.

Part V: Crossing the Bridge. Many times, the bridge has already been built by the time a librarian becomes involved in the process. Specifically, students come to the library with an assignment of which a librarian is unaware, or a librarian is asked to teach a class about the resources and services that will help students complete a specific assignment. The chapters in this section revolve around working with assignments that have already been created and distributed.

Of course there are times when nothing can be done to correct problems and make an assignment more effective. The final chapter offers a few suggestions for working and dealing with perennial problem assignments and the faculty members who distribute them.

In writing this book, I geared my comments and suggestions primarily to librarians who are relatively new to the profession or who don't work with students or faculty on a regular basis. These librarians often have little or no experience working with faculty or with the curriculum or with providing instruction. I was a member of this group when I became a librarian and wish I'd had a book of this nature to assist me with what has taken me years to learn through various on-the-job experiences and working in higher education. That said, although a good portion of what I've written may seem self-evident to more seasoned librarians, it is my hope that all librarians will find something of use in what they read.

I also made a conscious attempt to avoid redundancy. For example, the problem of requiring students to use a resource that isn't available isn't specific to a particular type of assignment. Many of the problems and suggestions discussed in this book apply to virtually any assignment. So, as you read, be aware of and reflect upon how these ideas and suggestions might apply to other assignments and specific scenarios in your library or on your campus.

Lastly, although this book is geared primarily toward librarians, I suspect (and hope) it might be read by faculty members as well. Faculty members who see their assignments used as examples or suspect a discussion point is directed at them should not take offense. They should rest assured that this is not an indictment against them or an indication that their assignments are bad. The point is that we're all on the same team and need to work together to create effective assignments that produce the desired learning outcomes for students to be successful in the classroom and beyond.

In the end, it's nice to imagine a world where information literacy is embedded into the entire curriculum (for both students and faculty); where librarians are involved with the development, administration, and evaluation of assignments; and where faculty and librarians interact and collaborate with each other on a regular and frequent basis. That day is peeking above the horizon for many of us. For now, it is my desire that this book will in some way become one more girder in the bridge that will take us into that new world.

PART I THE NEED FOR BRIDGES
Creating a Context for Success

ONE INFORMATION LITERACY AND THE NEED FOR EFFECTIVE ASSIGNMENTS

THE CONCEPT OF INFORMATION LITERACY (IL) can provide a useful framework for creating and ultimately evaluating the effectiveness of assignments. And yet, there are many challenges to understanding IL. Arguably, one of the biggest challenges is the simple fact that there are several interpretations and models of IL. This lack of a common language can create obstacles when librarians try to speak with faculty members about IL and its incorporation into their assignments.

That said, most definitions and interpretations are built upon the description offered in the final report of the American Library Association's Presidential Committee on Information Literacy. Issued in January 1989, the report characterizes an information literate individual as follows:

> Ultimately, information literate people are those who have learned how to learn. They know how to learn because they know how knowledge is organized, how to find information, and how to use information in such a way that others can learn from them. They are people prepared for life-long learning, because they can always find the information needed for any task or decision at hand.

For higher education, this description has since evolved into a series of standards. Proposed and adopted by the board of directors of the Association of College and Research Libraries (ACRL) in 2000, these standards are fully articulated in "Information Literacy Competency Standards for Higher Education" and are included in appendix A. References throughout the remainder of this book to what it means for an individual to be information literate should be read in the context of those standards. A student who is information literate

1. Determines the nature and extent of information needed

2. Accesses the needed information effectively and efficiently

3. Evaluates information and its sources critically and incorporates selected information into his or her knowledge base and value system

4. Individually or as a member of a group, uses information effectively to accomplish a specific purpose

5. Understands many of the economic, legal, and social issues surrounding the use of information and accesses and uses information ethically and legally

Instructors should attempt to incorporate these principles into their assignments whenever possible. Some assignments (e.g., term papers) may incorporate more of them than others. Some instructors or assignments may focus more on some elements than others. A lot depends on which type of instruction model is in place, the objectives of the course or assignment, and the individual professor's expectations and needs. In any case, the more closely aligned an assignment is with one or more of these principles, the more likely it will be to provide a meaningful and worthwhile learning experience for students and faculty alike.

THE NEED FOR EFFECTIVE ASSIGNMENTS

The need for students and graduates alike who can successfully work with and manage information continues to grow. The collaboration of librarians and faculty to create effective library assignments is an important and vital step in helping to meet this emergent and growing need. As alluded to in the introduction, on one level the rationale behind creating effective assignments is somewhat self-evident. Faculty expect students to complete an assignment as intended and with the expected results. And yet, changes in both society and higher education necessitate that these expectations be examined more deeply.

At a societal level, we are quickly evolving from the industrial age to an information or knowledge age. Boekhorst and Britz cite three common themes characterizing this new age. First, information has become one of the most important assets of society. Second, the focus is increasingly changing from acting upon the scarcity of information to managing the abundance of information. Third, the "rapid development of information and communication technologies has become the engine in the process of globalization" (2004, 63). As a result, the information age requires workers to possess a variety of new skills, and the need for and desirability of information skills is well documented (e.g., Breivik 2005; Dolence and Norris 1995; Doyle 1994; Gumport and Chun 2005).

This so-called knowledge economy is forcing a similar transformation in higher education. Like their public school counterparts a century ago, today's colleges and universities are under increasing pressure to provide practical knowledge and vocational skills. Students, parents, funding agencies, administrators, and more have growing expectations for accountability in higher education. In part, this is reflected in recent changes in the accreditation standards of various accrediting agencies. In talking about accreditation mandates and what they mean for faculty and librarians, Gary Thompson observes that "accrediting bodies have been moving in the direction of requiring greater accountability from institutions of higher education to ensure that students are learning and that students acquire the competencies to function effectively after graduation" (2002, 220).

In this new climate, growing attention is being devoted to the notion of IL because it provides a vehicle for addressing the provision of many of these competencies. The first specific mention of information literacy by a regional accrediting agency was in the 1994 edition of Middle States' *Characteristics of Excellence in Higher Education*. The reference was based on the ALA definition. Today, of the six regional accrediting agencies, three directly mention information literacy in their standards, and the other three refer to library instruction in a similar capacity. Although IL is still not a specified standard, it is clear that it is needed to achieve standards, and many colleges and universities have begun to restructure their curricula accordingly.

WHAT IS INFORMATION LITERACY?

What exactly is *information literacy*, and how is it related to working with faculty to create effective assignments involving the library? To answer these questions, it is helpful to place the concept in context by briefly looking at the development of the term itself and how it relates to instruction. To do so, it is important to first note that there are any number of models for and interpretations of IL. Appendix B provides a broad overview of some of the defining moments in the evolution of the concept.

Paul Zurkowski is generally credited (e.g., Behrens 1994; Boekhorst and Britz 2004; Grassian and Kaplowitz 2001) with coining the term *information literacy* back in 1974. Since then, the literature about what the term means and how it should be defined has continued to grow. As noted earlier, most existent models build upon the one developed by the ALA in the late 1980s. Because that model essentially revolves around locating, retrieving, evaluating, and using information in an ethical and legal manner, it provides an ideal context for discussing and understanding assignments. It can also serve as a useful framework for working with faculty to develop new assignments as well as to improve existing ones. And yet, librarians often face many challenges when attempting to create IL initiatives or otherwise trying to incorporate principles of IL into the curriculum, courses, or specific assignments. Some of these challenges are outlined in table 1.1.

WHAT IS LIBRARY INSTRUCTION?

The lack of a clear, universal definition for IL also tends to interfere with faculty understanding of what is meant by *information literacy instruction* and the role of librarians in the provision of such. Terms like *library orientation, bibliographic instruction,* and *user education,* for example, have long been used by librarians and others to denote instruction in the use of library resources. With the advent of IL, though, such terms have increasingly come to be used interchangeably with *information literacy instruction* (e.g., Grassian and Kaplowitz 2001; McCrank 1992; Salony 1995).

However, most proponents suggest that true IL instruction is much broader, much more comprehensive than traditional forms of library instruction. One-shot workshops, for example, still have a role to play in helping students to complete assignments effectively, but a single workshop cannot possibly cover all parts of the information spectrum needed to succeed in today's knowledge economy. Information literacy needs to be embedded into the entire curriculum and be the

TABLE 1.1   COMMON OBSTACLES TO INCORPORATING INFORMATION LITERACY INTO THE CURRICULUM

ISSUE	RESULTANT PROBLEMS
The literature on IL is often restricted to the library and information science fields.	• Those outside the library and information science fields often have minimal or unclear understanding of IL. • IL is perceived as a topic of importance primarily to librarians.
IL is an abstract concept.	• The abstract nature of IL makes it difficult to articulate exactly what is meant when someone is said to be information literate.
IL is equated with concepts such as critical thinking, resource-based learning, and lifelong learning.	• IL is seen as redundant, as something that's already being done, and, therefore, unnecessary. • IL is perceived as something extra that needs to be done.
IL is considered an umbrella term incorporating other kinds of literacy.	• Advocates of other types of literacy (e.g., visual, computer) resist being lumped together and see their fields as separate and distinct from IL. • Other literacies are assumed to be subordinate or inferior to information literacy.
IL is seen as a library thing.	• IL is regarded as relevant only to librarians. • Responsibility for IL instruction is attributed solely to librarians.

responsibility of everyone from all departments—not just the domain of the library or the librarians.

It is not surprising that the evolution of IL instruction in many ways parallels the growth and development of the notion of IL. Similarly, many of the challenges to understanding IL also present roadblocks to effective instruction. There are basically three models for incorporating principles of IL into the curriculum:

1. *Integrated:* built into an assignment, a course, a major, a discipline, or a university-wide initiative

2. *Nonintegrated:* presented through independent, self-contained credit or noncredit courses

3. *Hybrid:* combined into a blend of integrated and nonintegrated elements

How and to what degree instruction in the principles of IL is provided in each of these models varies. The types of instruction provided by libraries and librarians are summarized in table 1.2. In the table the emphases and assignments are matched to the type of instruction with which they are most commonly associated, but that does not mean that they are specific to that type only or that they are the sole emphases and assignments related to that type. Appendix C provides a more detailed time line of instruction in libraries.

ROLE OF IL IN CREATING BETTER ASSIGNMENTS

The principles of IL provide a useful tool that can be used to both create and evaluate assignments. The problem lies in creating assignments that successfully address these principles. At the core of doing so are three basic questions that need to be addressed:

1. Which standards, indicators, or outcomes is the assignment designed to address?

2. How will the principles manifest in the assignment?

3. How will the principles be assessed?

Success in addressing these and related questions will ultimately be reflected in the quality of work generated by students as well as the overall quality of the learning experience. The remainder of this chapter demonstrates how the ACRL standards can be used as a framework for creating effective assignments.

NEED: Is the Assignment Sufficiently Described?

For most assignments, the final product is clear and straightforward. However, sometimes faculty do not clearly articulate specific details or assume students know what's expected. But it's not enough to assign a term paper and only discuss expectations for things like formatting and length. Often assignments are rendered ineffective because of a failure to clearly delineate expectations about things such as whether or not it's acceptable to use websites as sources. Similarly, for a multipart assignment, when each part is scored separately and all the scores are combined into a total grade, students need to know which elements are worth more than others so that they can decide where to focus the most effort. When expectations aren't clearly defined, students have no way of assessing their strengths and weaknesses and determining how to improve their performance on the next assignment. The more details a faculty member can supply, the easier it will be for students and the librarian to work on completing the assignment successfully.

TABLE 1.2   LIBRARY INSTRUCTION MODELS

TYPE OF INSTRUCTION	EMERGED	EMPHASIS	CHARACTERISTIC ASSIGNMENT
Library orientation	Pre-1900	Location and availability of various resources and services	• Tour • Scavenger hunt
Library instruction	Pre-WWII	"How do I _____?"	• Essay/research project • Term paper
Course integration	Post-WWII	Specific, assignment-based needs	Varies by course and by professor
Credit-bearing courses	1960s	Broad cross section of topics related to libraries and information	Varies to reflect needs and expectations of professor, course, discipline, school, or university
IL instruction	1980s	Embedded into entire curriculum; process-based, collaborative models increasingly commonplace	Varies to reflect needs and expectations of professor, course, discipline, school, or university
Looking ahead	21st century	Growing need for information literate students who can efficiently and effectively use emergent information technologies	Varies to reflect needs and expectations of professor, course, discipline, school, or university

ACCESS: Are Adequate Resources and Services Available and Accessible?

It is important to ensure that students have access to the resources and services needed to complete a given assignment. The variety of needs can be endless. Admittedly, no library can have every possible resource or service or provide access to every possible source of information. Consequently, faculty members requiring students to use a particular resource or service must work with the librarians to ensure that it will be both available *and* accessible at the time the assignment is distributed.

RETRIEVE: Do Students Have the Skills Needed to Complete the Assignment?

Faculty need to be made aware that students possess a broad range of information and technology skills. The levels of these skills are equally varied. As a result, even when IL is embedded in the curriculum, students may still lack the skills needed to complete a particular assignment successfully. Moreover, even if they have the necessary skills, students may not know which resources to access to acquire the information they need or how to apply their skills to the current course or assignment.

EVALUATE: How and How Often Will the Assignment Be Evaluated?

Just because an assignment is effective one semester doesn't mean it will be so in the future. Assignments need to be monitored and updated on a regular basis. Changes to resources and services, the relocation of items, and changes in access methods are just some of the many things that can change at any time. Sometimes aspects of an assignment will need to be modified, and other times things will need to be added or removed. Too, content changes in the discipline, world events, and other factors can quickly render an assignment outdated or otherwise inappropriate. In short, librarians need to work with faculty on a frequent and regular basis to ensure that any given assignment is doable, accurate, and appropriate.

INCORPORATE: What Was Learned from the Assignment?

Another way of approaching an assignment is to ask if it is geared toward understanding a process or toward generating a product. For example, a process-oriented assignment may be developed with the expectation that students will learn how to do a literature review or cite sources, whereas a product-oriented assignment may be designed to have students generate or acquire additional content. In both cases, the assignments may be used to determine the degree to which students have achieved the expected learning outcome. Other measures, such as tests and quizzes, may also be used in this respect.

ACCOMPLISH: What Is the Purpose or Intended Outcome of the Assignment?

The success of a particular assignment is directly related to the clarity of its purpose or intended outcome. If neither the faculty member nor the librarian can clearly articulate the purpose of a given assignment or what kind of results are expected— either in terms of a final product or student learning—the assignment is doomed to be mediocre at best and busywork at worst. In both cases, the final product will almost certainly fall short of expectations, and the assignment's ability to produce a worthwhile learning experience will be severely compromised.

USE: What Are the Expectations regarding the Use of Information?

Students need to know the correct way to use and cite their sources as well as the penalties they'll incur if they do not. At the most basic level, point deductions for improper source use should be explicitly stated for each assignment. In addition, qualitative concerns need to be clearly addressed. For example, most faculty probably agree that plagiarizing is a far more serious offense than citing a source improperly. And yet, is all plagiarizing inherently wrong, or is there a difference between plagiarizing a sentence and plagiarizing an entire paragraph? Faculty members need to go beyond their own individual needs and expectations to ensure that they are aware of and enforce departmental, institutional, and societal/legal guidelines for the use of information.

A FINAL WORD . . .

Those new to instruction and even those who have been teaching a while will find it worthwhile to visit the ACRL's information literacy website: www.ala.org/ala/mgrps/ divs/acrl/issues/infolit/index.cfm. The site provides a wealth of information about IL and integrating it into the curriculum. Among the site's many useful pages can be found links to detailed discussions of the standards, performance indicators, and outcomes for the ACRL's "Information Literacy Competency Standards for Higher Education" (see appendix A). Information about modifying the standards for specific disciplines, collaboration, creating assignments, examples, and more can also be found on the site.

PART II BUILDING A FOUNDATION
Librarian-Faculty Collaboration

TWO WORKING WITH FACULTY AND THE CURRICULUM

THE NEED

The need for librarians to work with faculty to create and evaluate assignments cannot be overemphasized. Doing so would seem to be a relatively easy, straightforward task. After all, faculty and librarians alike are on the same team, working to educate students. And yet, it cannot be assumed that faculty will automatically be open to and willing to work with librarians to create better assignments. Many factors may contribute to faculty reluctance or resistance. Some of these can be overcome. However, some are inherent in higher education, and the best that can be hoped for is that their impact can be minimized. Either way, librarians need to be aware of these factors if they are to establish good, healthy librarian-faculty relationships. Lacking such a relationship, many faculty members will continue to develop assignments on their own, many of which will fall short of their intended goals and objectives.

THE BENEFITS

There are a number of advantages to working with a faculty member to create a good library assignment. Perhaps the most obvious is that the likelihood of surprises is minimized when students come to the library. That is, by being familiar with the assignment beforehand, librarians know what's expected. In turn, they are able to provide better assistance, which decreases librarian and student frustration and confusion and increases the quality of the finished product.

But the need for librarians to establish strong rapport with faculty members goes much deeper than simply working together on assignments. Librarians constantly need to remind themselves of three things.

First, faculty create the assignments that necessitate students' use of the library. The growing availability of remote access to resources and services has already reduced the need for many students to come to the library. A reduction in library-related assignments reduces this need even further. As a result, gate counts, circulation, the number of individuals seeking reference assistance, and other statistics continue to decline at many libraries. Although such measures do not always paint a clear picture of a library's usefulness, many administrators still use them as the primary metrics for establishing funding and making personnel decisions. Either way, each assignment or course that doesn't require the use of the library diminishes the value of the library and the role of the librarians.

Second, allowing librarians to provide library instruction is often the exception, not the rule. At many campuses, the courses that call for the use of library resources and services far outnumber the courses for which a librarian is asked to provide instruction. A growing number of faculty members are providing library instruction themselves. But, more often than not, faculty members are reluctant to give up an hour or two of class time. Given all of the discipline-specific content they are expected to deliver, many instructors are hesitant to relinquish precious class time for what they perceive as outside topics such as how to use library resources and services.

Third, faculty play a pivotal role in shaping student perceptions about the library and its usefulness for course work and for the future. If a faculty member doesn't create good library assignments, the perceived value of libraries and librarians as well as their many and varied resources and services will be marginal. At best, students may come to see the library as a confusing, frustrating place. At worst, students who are never exposed to using the library properly will be less likely to understand its value to them in the future.

ASSIGNMENT TRANSACTIONS

An assignment transaction is essentially the process by which an assignment is generated and completed. Every assignment transaction involving the library has two distinct though interrelated components. First, there is the life cycle of the assignment itself. Then there are the participants involved at any particular stage of the transaction.

Assignment Life Cycle

An assignment life cycle consists of the various stages of an assignment's lifetime. Figure 2.1 shows the four stages through which every assignment typically passes: development, distribution, completion, and evaluation.

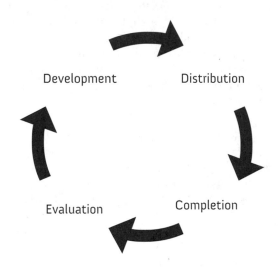

FIGURE 2.1   ASSIGNMENT LIFE CYCLE

It is important to observe that the process is cyclical. That is, during the evaluation stage, the strengths and weaknesses of an assignment are exposed, thereby enabling reasonable decisions to be made about how to modify the assignment before it's distributed again. With the development of those modifications, the process begins anew, and it continues indefinitely.

The evaluation phase of the life cycle helps faculty members to ensure their assignments are accomplishing their intended goals and objectives. Librarians have firsthand experience working with an assignment (i.e., during the completion stage). Therefore, they are in an excellent position to provide meaningful insight into what worked and what didn't.

Unfortunately, the evaluative component is often missed or not incorporated into many assignments. As a result, the process becomes linear, with distinct starting and ending points. Lacking the evaluative component, faculty members may be unaware of how their assignments failed and doom subsequent students to working on assignments that fall short of expectations. Some faculty members may blame the students, believing that the poor caliber of the finished product is the result of student negligence, laziness, or some other shortcoming rather than a flaw in the assignment itself. Even faculty members who are aware of problems with an assignment may not be aware of what caused the problems or how to correct them.

This suggests an even greater need for librarians to be involved in the entire life cycle of an assignment. Librarians are typically most heavily involved with stage three and, to a lesser degree, with stage two. Unfortunately, unless some sort of information component is embedded into the curriculum, librarians are often only minimally involved with steps one and four. Sometimes this is intentional. For whatever reasons, some librarians may choose not to participate in the development and evaluation of assignments. Many times, though, librarians don't have a choice. Faculty members may choose to create and evaluate assignments with little or no input from a librarian whatsoever. When this occurs, librarians are forced to work with any and all assignments that come their way. This leaves librarians in the dark about what's expected, which often translates into ineffective or inappropriate assistance for students trying to complete their assignments.

Dynamics of Participants' Transactions

In addition to understanding the assignment life cycle, it is equally important for librarians to be familiar with the participant dynamics present with any assignment transaction. When an assignment involves use of the library, there are three key participants: the faculty member, the student, and the librarian. The participants and their typical involvement in specific stages of the assignment life cycle are shown in table 2.1.

As can be seen in figure 2.2, the interaction of any two participants at any given stage of the assignment typically excludes the third participant. For example, a student is rarely, if ever, directly involved in the development of an assignment, whereas a faculty member is typically exempt from the completion stage. As evidenced by the darker area where the three circles intersect, the important thing to keep in mind is that *all* participants in *every* transaction interact with the assignment on *some* level. Both the level and the degree of involvement with the assignment will vary for each participant and with each assignment.

Several key points should be kept in mind with regard to the dynamics among the participants in an assignment transaction.

TABLE 2.1   PARTICIPANTS' INVOLVEMENT IN ASSIGNMENT LIFE CYCLE

PARTICIPANT	DEVELOPMENT	DISTRIBUTION	COMPLETION	EVALUATION
Faculty	X	X		X
Student			X	
Librarian		X	X	

FIGURE 2.2   INTERACTIONS BETWEEN ASSIGNMENT PARTICIPANTS

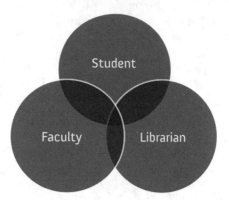

Faculty-Student Dynamic

Although there are certainly exceptions, as a rule librarians have little direct involvement with the faculty-student dynamic. Still, there are a couple of key issues that librarians should be aware of when working with students completing assignments.

Students may feel uncomfortable asking their instructor questions about an assignment. Because librarians typically don't grade assignments, they are often perceived as neutral and objective. Thus, students may feel more comfortable speaking with a librarian than with their professor. However, both the student and the librarian should be careful to avoid overinterpreting an assignment. The faculty member should *always* be consulted for definitive answers to questions about an assignment.

Students may not have the opportunity to provide feedback about their assignments. Here again, librarians can be the students' best advocate. Students are rarely asked to provide feedback on most assignments. Feedback, if sought, is often limited to content-related questions (e.g., What did you learn?) and does not touch on structural or administrative aspects of the assignment. As noted earlier, when problems do arise, students themselves are sometimes seen as being at fault. In those instances, it is incumbent on librarians to speak with the faculty members and alert them to the fact that problems resulted from some aspect of the assignment and not (necessarily) from the students.

Librarian-Student Dynamic

How a librarian responds to requests for assistance not only shapes the way students complete their assignments but also plays a critical role in shaping students' views of librarians and of libraries as a whole. To that end, several points need mentioning.

Every student's question is unique and deserves an answer. Even in instances where a class has been given instruction from a librarian, there are likely to be questions. It's important to keep in mind that even though the same question may have been asked by every student in the class, each student has asked the question only once. Although the answers to some questions may seem obvious to the librarian, they are not obvious to the person asking them. If an answer *were* obvious, there would be no need to ask the question. In short, every question should be treated as legitimate and of significance to the person asking it.

Librarians need to wear different hats for different students. Everyone's needs and interests are unique. Obviously, a primary role for librarians is providing assignment assistance. This often involves more than just directing students to a particular resource or teaching them how to search a database. For example, librarians often help with things such as topic development and provide insight into how to properly cite sources. Many times, though, students merely need someone who will listen— whether about an assignment or something else entirely.

Students may not feel a rapport with librarians. Simply put, some students may not feel comfortable asking a librarian for assistance for any number of reasons. For instance, they may have received poor service in the past, they may be shy or otherwise uncomfortable about asking for assistance, or they may not know that a librarian can help them. Librarians shouldn't take this personally. They should, however, work to become aware of potential barriers and work to ensure they are minimized.

Librarian-Assignment Dynamic

There is a direct relationship between librarians' familiarity with an assignment and their ability to provide effective and meaningful assistance. Because of such, it is important to be aware of the various stages of assignment awareness as outlined in table 2.2. Note that at all four levels—even at full familiarity—a librarian may still misinterpret what exactly a student needs or wants.

THE CHALLENGES

Librarians at many institutions struggle to gain a foothold with faculty. The success or failure of librarians in this respect is dependent on a number of factors. Some of the obstacles are easier to overcome than others. Still, librarians wishing to develop strong working relationships with faculty members need to be aware that doing so will not necessarily be a smooth or easy task.

The role of librarians in the educational process is often misunderstood or overlooked. Faculty attitudes toward libraries and librarians can be a significant hurdle. Many librarians, for example, are not perceived as being involved in the curriculum or in the educational process. As a result, librarians are not valued for the contributions they can and do make. The lack of faculty status for many librarians only exacerbates this perception, as does the inability of many faculty members (and students) to distinguish between staff members and librarians. Many are unclear about or have a very limited understanding of what a librarian does and often mistakenly believe that librarians merely sign out books and otherwise spend the majority of their days reading.

TABLE 2.2 LEVELS OF ASSIGNMENT AWARENESS

AMOUNT OF FAMILIARITY	FACULTY EXPECTATIONS AND ASSIGNMENT GOALS	ASSIGNMENT AWARENESS	
		Student	*Librarian*
None	• Unstated • Clarification required to complete assignment effectively	• Lacks knowledge or ability to articulate specific assignment needs	• Lacks knowledge of assignment until student asks for assistance
Vague	• Poorly stated • Subject to misunderstanding or misinterpretation	• Lacks copy of assignment but describes general needs	• Has indirect (e.g., word-of-mouth) knowledge of assignment • Has worked with *previous* iterations of assignment • Has not discussed assignment with faculty or other librarians
Moderate	• Initially indistinct but can be clarified by reviewing assignment	• Presents copy of assignment when asking for assistance	• Has worked with *current* iteration of assignment • Has discussed assignment with faculty or other librarians *after* its distribution
Full	• Precisely stated • Instructor and librarian collaborate in developing assignment	• Before asking for assistance, has copy of precisely worded assignment, as does librarian	• Has worked with *current* iteration of assignment *and* • Has discussed assignment with faculty or other librarians *before* its distribution

Librarians don't have a monopoly on information or on teaching students to work with it. Librarians can be their own worst enemies. Many librarians believe—consciously or not—that their training in the organization, access, and use of information makes them more qualified than nonlibrarians to talk about topics related to the library and information. However, if librarians expect faculty members to work with them, librarians have to be open to the idea that they no longer have a monopoly on information or on teaching students how to work effectively with information.

Professors must often choose between research/publication and teaching. Traditionally, the role of faculty members has been that of disseminators of knowledge. This can be done through teaching, research, and publication. Unfortunately, developments in society and in higher education have tended to focus faculty efforts on the latter two at the expense of the first. Moreover, the majority of faculty members have never been taught how to teach. Although all develop subject expertise, few graduate programs incorporate courses on topics like learning theory and teaching strategies that faculty members can use to convey content more effectively to their students.

Professional demands on time make it difficult for faculty to meet with librarians. The lack of time is a multifaceted problem that's not easily addressed. Higher education revolves around committee work and meetings. The latter can consume a lot of time. As a result, faculty members may have only a limited window of opportunity to meet with a librarian. Some faculty members may be able to squeeze in one meeting, but because little can be accomplished in so short a time, they may forgo meeting at all.

Limitations on classroom time make it difficult to include library instruction. Most classes are still administered in a fifty-minute or seventy-five-minute format. When a librarian is asked to make a presentation during a single class period, it is difficult to cover anything more than the basics. However, librarians must recognize that it is even more difficult for faculty to give up class time for a series of sessions in library instruction. Just as librarians feel that fifty minutes is not enough time to convey all the information students need to use the library effectively, faculty members may feel that a full term is not enough time to cover all the information they need to present. This is not to say that faculty members don't appreciate the value of a presentation by a librarian. It simply means they don't feel they can relinquish even a single class period if they're to adequately get through their content.

An institution's governance structure may make it difficult to achieve institutional changes. In higher education, consensus is the predominant model of decision making. Reaching a consensus on any issue, though, is often a time-consuming and laborious process. It is not uncommon that an issue must pass through several committees before action of any kind is taken. This is particularly true at larger institutions or institutions where the faculty members are unionized.

The curriculum process may limit what a faculty member can and can't do with a course. How curriculum issues are addressed varies from campus to campus. Many institutions have a campuswide curriculum committee. Most institutions have some form of departmental curriculum committees as well. Although faculty members may be open to changes, it may not be within their power to modify a course or assignment. Even if it is, they may not feel comfortable making changes without consulting the appropriate committees.

Faculty may resist sharing or even discussing elements of their courses. Faculty have both the right and the responsibility to determine a significant portion (if not all) of the content, objectives, outcomes, and so on for the courses they teach. This belief in professional autonomy is firmly entrenched in higher education and is not conducive to sharing teaching responsibilities. When approached about changing their assignments or other elements of their courses, many faculty members will resist, feeling their academic freedom is being encroached upon.

Some individuals are more resistant to change than others. Resistance to change is likely to be found on personal, professional, and institutional levels. Whereas some people are just not open to change, many others are. However, a number of mitigating factors may temper the degree to which they attempt to effect change. Nontenured faculty and faculty up for promotion, for example, may be particularly uncomfortable making changes to their courses or assignments. Institutional priorities, lack of funding, and a host of other factors might also create significant roadblocks to change.

Many faculty members may be unaware of what assistance the library has to offer. Many faculty members may not be aware of the types and levels of assistance the library and librarians can provide to them and their students. They may be even less aware of which person in the library to contact about instruction- and assignment-related issues.

Faculty members may not feel comfortable approaching a librarian for assistance. Many libraries assign librarians to work with specific departments on things like collection development and instruction. Often these assignments are based on the particular subject expertise or background of the librarian. Just as often, though, the assignments are arbitrary. If no liaison is in place, a faculty member may not be comfortable approaching an unknown librarian to discuss instruction- and assignment-related issues. If liaisons are in place, they may have limited experience with instruction or minimal interest in discussing assignments.

Even if the liaison does have the interest or experience, a faculty member may feel another librarian is better suited to the situation. However, the faculty member may be hesitant about contacting the other librarian for fear of causing harsh feelings. Conversely, a librarian may be capable of working with an instructor or a department but be unwilling or unable to do so for fear of stepping on the toes of a fellow librarian and compromising their working relationship.

WAYS TO GET INVOLVED

Everyone is busy. Budget cutbacks, increased workloads, and other factors are forcing people to do more with less in virtually all levels of higher education. For these and other reasons, librarians are not alone in sometimes feeling uncomfortable

devoting time and effort to activities that do not directly benefit them, their department, or their library. And yet, to be successful in working with a faculty member
to create effective assignments, a librarian needs to establish a collaborative atmosphere and a positive, healthy relationship with that faculty member.

Approachability is a key factor in this respect. Faculty members who are uncomfortable approaching a librarian are less likely to feel comfortable forming a working
relationship. They will be even less likely to be open to critiques of their assignments
or to act on any suggestions a librarian might make. In fact, they may perceive such
critiques as intrusive, mean-spirited, or worse. In response, they may be reluctant
to schedule library instruction or to refer students to that librarian. They may even
avoid having students use the library at all.

Opening the lines of communication is a critical first step in creating a more
collaborative, professional atmosphere in which faculty members and librarians
alike feel comfortable working together. The following are just a handful of the
many ways librarians can develop their approachability and otherwise become more
involved with faculty and the curriculum.

Be seen around campus. Being able to put a name to a face is a huge part of
approachability. On a professional level, getting involved with campus committees
and other academic activities is a great way to gain exposure to a broad cross section
of the faculty. But, even on a personal level, attending campus sporting and cultural
events, eating lunch with faculty members, and participating in activities at which
faculty are likely to be present are simple ways for librarians to become more recog-
nizable and, ultimately, more approachable.

Get involved with or start a liaison program. The roles of library liaisons vary.
Many libraries assign librarians to work with specific departments. In this case, the
liaison is typically responsible for addressing all of the departments' library-related
needs, from acquiring items for the collection to providing instruction for those
departments. In other models, though, the roles of the liaisons are based upon specific functions or sets of duties. For example, some librarians may be designated
collection liaisons and work with all departments on collection development. Other
librarians may act as instruction liaisons and work with all departments on instruction. Regardless, the core of a liaison program revolves around providing means for
libraries to promote their resources and services and for faculty to have a contact
person with whom to work.

Attend departmental meetings. The most obvious benefits of attending departmental meetings are saving time and increasing clarity. It's a lot more effective to
speak with everyone at once rather than individually. It also ensures that everyone
gets the same information. More than that, though, attending departmental meetings
enables librarians to become familiar with faculty and shows a willingness to work
with them. It is a great way to keep in touch with a department's needs and interests,
which can be extremely useful in terms of collection development and instruction.

Create and participate in professional development activities for faculty. Most
library programming is focused on students. Unfortunately, similar programs for

faculty are noticeably absent at many libraries for any number of reasons (e.g., lack of time and resources), and the programs that do exist were often developed without faculty input. Because many librarians are not considered faculty, they are not invited or are unaware of professional development activities for faculty. However, a lack of invitations should not be taken as a sign that librarians would not be welcome—either as presenters or as attendees. Every campus is different, but some of the more common ways in which librarians could participate in professional development activities for faculty include

- being a presenter at (new) faculty orientation
- attending faculty retreats
- asking to be on the agenda for faculty in-service days or meetings
- participating in their institution's Center for Teaching Excellence (or its equivalent)

Get involved in curriculum development. Librarians may participate in curriculum development at the departmental level or at the campus level. This can be a lot of work, but it can also yield the greatest rewards and generate credibility and clout for librarians. The philosophical and practical goals and objectives of a curriculum are developed at the departmental level. Librarians who become involved from the very start gain crucial knowledge that equips them to provide the most appropriate instruction in using the library.

Being involved at the institutional level has numerous benefits as well. Doing so gives librarians both a chance to meet faculty from a broad cross section of the campus community and firsthand knowledge of new courses or programs being developed. By seeing syllabi and other course materials, librarians become familiar with what's expected and can work to develop and improve assignments accordingly.

DISCUSSING PROBLEMATIC ASSIGNMENTS

Arguably among the hardest decisions a librarian must make is when it is (and is not) appropriate to contact a faculty member about an ineffective assignment. If nothing is done, there is a real risk that generations of students will be frustrated and confused about both the assignment and the library. However, suggesting to faculty members that an assignment can't be completed as instructed or is in any way deficient is likely to place them on the defensive. This is exacerbated when strong librarian-faculty rapport has not been cultivated in the first place.

In addition, contacting a faculty member may force librarians to deal with personal issues. That is, maybe it's not the assignment but the librarian's ability to provide appropriate assistance that's the problem. Many librarians are reluctant to admit or don't even consider that they may have contributed to the failure of an assignment. There are any of a number of reasons for such. The point is that some librarians may avoid contacting a faculty member because they don't want to share the blame for a failed assignment.

Ultimately, every librarian needs to do a sort of cost-benefit analysis before contacting a faculty member about a problematic assignment. That is, librarians need to determine if the possible benefits outweigh the potential difficulties such contact might generate. The following are some of the many questions to consider when making such decisions about problems with assignments.

Who Is the Best Person to Initiate the Contact?

Every library is different. In most instances, the librarian working with students who are having problems with an assignment would seem to be the most obvious choice to contact the faculty member because that librarian has firsthand knowledge of the situation. And yet, the choice isn't always as straightforward as it might seem. One of the key shortcomings of this approach is that librarians typically rotate shifts at the reference desk throughout the day. As a result, several librarians may be unaware that others have experienced the same problem. If multiple librarians call the faculty member about the same problem, the number and variety of calls may seem more like a full-fledged attack than a well-intentioned attempt at positive feedback.

This is one of the advantages of having a surrogate contact faculty members. Some libraries, for example, have designated instruction librarians responsible for working with curricular matters. These individuals may be more knowledgeable about pedagogical methods and concerns. In libraries where librarians serve as liaisons to specific departments, those librarians often have established working relationships with faculty members. Because they are not seen as outsiders, they may be more comfortable and, ultimately, more successful in contacting faculty members about assignment problems.

Table 2.3 summarizes some of the relative advantages and disadvantages of both approaches.

Suggestions
- Work within the structure of your library.
- Adopt an agreed-upon problem-reporting procedure as a means of eliminating duplicate contacts.

What Is the Best Way to Contact a Faculty Member?

There are a variety of ways to approach a faculty member, each with its own distinct set of advantages and disadvantages. Librarians have to decide which method is most appropriate. The value of personal interaction in relation to the amount of time involved needs to be considered. A librarian's ability to generate a response from a faculty member depends on the level and degree of the instructor's involvement in the completion phase of the assignment, the nature of the faculty-librarian dynamic, and, of course, the instructor's availability. When a student is standing at the reference desk asking for immediate assistance, the librarian has no time to schedule a face-to-face meeting with the instructor. Even if the librarian tries to contact the instructor while the student stands by, there is no guarantee that the instructor will be available to answer questions. In the end, a combination of approaches may be best. Table 2.4 outlines the relative advantages and disadvantages of some common means of interacting with faculty members about assignments.

Suggestions

- Weigh the necessary response time against the efficacy of a face-to-face meeting with a faculty member and act accordingly.
- Know your own personal strengths and weaknesses in communicating and working with a faculty member or a department to improve a problematic assignment.
- Once contact is initiated, be extremely careful to keep identifying details (e.g., a student's name) out of the conversation.

TABLE 2.3   DECIDING WHO SHOULD CONTACT FACULTY MEMBERS

PERSON MAKING CONTACT	ADVANTAGES	DISADVANTAGES
Librarian who has observed problem	• Has firsthand knowledge of problem • Can provide immediate assistance if faculty member is available	• May not be comfortable or qualified to discuss problem • May not be aware that other librarians have already made contact • May have no or poor relationship with faculty member
Surrogate identified by the library	• May be well equipped to discuss content (e.g., liaison) or pedagogical concerns (e.g., instruction librarian) • May have working relationship with faculty member or department • Essentially eliminates possibility of duplicate contacts	• May have no or poor relationship with faculty member or department • Risks being perceived as passing the buck by both faculty member and other librarians • May take time to be contacted and brought up-to-date, which delays contact with faculty member

When Should Contact Be Made?

Some problems are more urgent than others. As a rule, problems that prevent a student from properly completing an assignment should be reported as quickly as possible so that as many students as possible can be helped. Some issues, though, may take longer to resolve. Broader pedagogical concerns (e.g., unclear goals and expectations) may not be resolvable in a single quick phone call. Establishing a meeting to discuss such problems may take several days or even weeks.

Suggestions

- Develop an effective method of triage to determine which problems need to be addressed immediately (i.e., those that prevent students from properly completing the assignment) and which are more long-term in nature (e.g., instructional goals) and can be addressed in the future.
- Establish a calendar of weekly, monthly, term, or annual meetings at which assignment concerns can be discussed with faculty members.

How Many Difficulties Make an Assignment Problematic?

Determining the point at which an assignment becomes problematic has at least two facets. The first is the actual number of errors an assignment contains. Few would

TABLE 2.4   MEANS OF CONTACTING FACULTY MEMBERS ABOUT ASSIGNMENT PROBLEMS

MEANS OF CONTACT	ADVANTAGES	DISADVANTAGES
Indirect (e.g., e-mail, phone)	• Can initiate contact immediately • Possibility of immediate response	• Impersonal • May not yield quick response • Easy to misinterpret what's written or said in a message • May require repeated follow-up and clarification • Faculty member may lack time or interest to respond indirectly
Direct (i.e., face-to-face)	• Extremely personal • Allows for dialogue	• Takes time to coordinate meeting • May be seen as confrontational • May put faculty member on defensive • Librarian may have no or poor relationship with faculty member

argue that it is worthwhile to contact faculty members over a single typographical error. And yet, there may be instances in which a single error warrants contacting the faculty member. For example, an incomplete or inaccurate citation may make it difficult or even impossible for students to complete an assignment.

The second and arguably more significant aspect of this issue revolves around the number of times a problem has been experienced. Here librarians have to use their best judgment. Five students having difficulty out of a class of ten, for example, seems more significant than five students out of a class of thirty. Regardless of the number of students experiencing problems, though, librarians need to consider that there may be other factors contributing to their difficulties. For example, maybe the students missed an important class or weren't paying attention when their professor answered students' questions about the assignment. In addition, given that only students with problems typically ask for assistance, there may be a sizable silent majority who are not experiencing any problems whatsoever. In short, librarians should exercise caution about assuming that when a given number of students ask for help, there must be a problem with the assignment.

Suggestions
- Pick your battles wisely.
- Be certain that the problem is directly related to the assignment and not caused by students' personal problems or an instructor's personal preferences (e.g., font selection).

Why Should a Faculty Member Listen to a Librarian?

Librarians and faculty members alike want students to succeed. Because of this and because librarians are an integral part of the educational process, they have a right *and* a responsibility to try to improve students' educational experience. When presented in a nonconfrontational, collaborative context, assignment feedback is welcomed by most faculty members. Feedback not only helps to improve assignments for future students but also paves the way for stronger librarian–faculty-member relationships. But it's crucial to tread lightly. Some faculty members immediately become defensive about any critique of their work, particularly if they feel that the criticisms are unwarranted or that the concerns are unfounded or inconsequential. Librarians may be seen as outsiders who lack the knowledge or expertise to critique assignments. When pushed, some faculty members may even defend a bad assignment by citing academic freedom and professional autonomy.

Suggestions
- Remain positive and emphasize that we're all playing for the same team.
- *Never* personalize your concerns. Work to ensure that any and all criticisms and discussions remain professional in nature. Do not let personal biases about the assignment or the faculty member cloud your judgment about an assignment.

Why Should a Librarian Listen to a Faculty Member?

Because librarians are often only minimally involved in the classroom experience (if at all), they are often unaware of the specific context of an assignment and how it fits into the overall scope of the course. That is, librarians encountering an assignment typically have not heard the corresponding lectures or seen the other assignments that students are expected to complete throughout the term. Sometimes, for example, a student who is having difficulty with a current assignment may not have completed a previous assignment correctly. Certainly problems should be brought to the attention of faculty members. However, except when an assignment is clearly at fault (e.g., a required resource isn't available in the library), librarians should ultimately yield to a faculty member's vision, experience, and judgment.

Suggestions

- Don't lose sight of the fact that the course for which a problematic assignment has been made is the province of the faculty member, not yours.
- Do not assume that you are always right or that your approach or suggestion is necessarily an improvement.
- Keep in mind that, with few exceptions, you will typically have far less content knowledge or expertise than faculty members.
- Librarians often have far less teaching experience overall and less varied teaching experience than classroom faculty members do.

WHEN ASSIGNMENTS FAIL

No one likes to fail, especially if there is a way to prevent the failure. And yet, despite their best intentions and no matter what they do or try, librarians need to be prepared for the occasional failure. There are some faculty members, for example, who will never schedule an IL instruction session for their students or learn how to use library resources themselves. Consequently, their students come to the library completely unprepared to do the work needed to complete an assignment. Other faculty members will resist hearing about problems with an assignment and discussing how best to help students in the future. As a result, the same faulty assignment shows up term after term. A few faculty members may even tout student difficulties as a badge of honor in that "research isn't supposed to be easy." They attribute difficulties to students' shortcomings or inexperience and not to the weakness of the assignment itself.

Simply put, although it's usually not the norm, there will be times when a librarian is unable to establish rapport and work with a faculty member to create effective assignments. Unfortunately, with some assignments, there will be little or nothing that can be done. In these instances, librarians can only resign themselves to the inevitable and accept that an assignment has failed. Table 2.5 highlights four common reasons that an assignment may fail due to lack of collaboration or poor librarian-faculty relations.

Suggestions

- When working with a student, minimize negative responses—whether verbal and nonverbal—to both the assignment and the professor.
- Do what you think is best in terms of helping the student in need.
- Be sure you inform students when you're making a judgment call about an assignment as well as the possible consequences of following your advice (e.g., a lower grade). Then let the students decide which direction to take—right or wrong and regardless of feelings you may have to the contrary.
- Do not take failed assignments personally.
- Be sure you contact faculty members about problems with their assignments but don't harass them. At some point, accept that nothing can or will be done and make a conscious decision to move on.
- Contact the appropriate department chairperson, dean, curriculum committee, or the provost. However, this should only be done in extreme cases. Even when you know you're justified and are 100 percent on target with your observations and suggestions, the fallout from doing this sort of end run may ultimately cause more problems than it solves and almost guarantees personalizing the problem.
- See chapter 13 for additional insight into how to deal with ineffective assignments.

TABLE 2.5   COMMON REASONS ASSIGNMENTS FAIL

FAILURE	DESCRIPTION
Students are ill prepared	Students don't know what's expected or don't have skills needed to complete assignment
Assignment contains flaws	Elements of assignment cannot be completed or do not yield expected results
Flawed assignment is repeated	Faulty assignment continues to be distributed every time the professor teaches the course
Librarian lacks rapport with faculty member	Faculty member is resistant to discussing assignment or difficulties students experienced while completing it

PART III BUILDING THE BRIDGE
Developing Effective Library Assignments

THREE COMMON REASONS ASSIGNMENTS FAIL

AN ASSIGNMENT INVOLVING THE LIBRARY can fall short for any of a number of reasons. Some of these are assignment-specific, but others are broader, more universal. This chapter focuses on the latter group. As they are not necessarily related to the content or structure of the assignments themselves, these flaws are often more subtle and are easily overlooked. Assignment-specific issues and concerns will be dealt with in chapters 4 through 10.

To better explore the general issues and their impact on assignments, this chapter is split into two parts. "The Big Three" discusses three of the most common reasons assignments may fail to meet desired expectations. These issues cut across all disciplines and assignment types.

The remainder of the chapter presents an overview of some of the other common problems and shortcomings that may occur in assignments. These are grouped loosely into two broad categories: administrative issues and perceptual issues. Administrative flaws impede a student's ability to complete an assignment. Perceptual shortcomings stem from misperceptions faculty members may have about students, the library, or the research process that interfere with students' ability to complete the assignment as desired.

THE BIG THREE

There are any of a number of factors that contribute to an assignment's falling short of expectations. Some of these factors are course-specific or assignment-specific. However, there are three factors—the Big Three—that are universal in that they may affect any and all assignments:

1. Tacit or unclear purpose

2. Unclear, dated, or inappropriate terminology

3. Missing resources or limited resource access

Tacit or Unclear Purpose

Every assignment should have a well-defined *and* well-articulated purpose. When an assignment falls short in this respect, a lack of explicit purpose may be at fault. Sometimes the purpose of an assignment may be poorly worded, or the way the instructor characterizes the assignment in class may be vague or assumed to be tacitly understood. As a result, how students interpret and ultimately complete the assignment may differ significantly from the faculty member's goals and expectations.

In a worst-case scenario, an assignment may not have a stated purpose at all. Then, rather than focusing on the process and the desired learning experience, students quickly shift to focusing on the product and getting the assignment completed. Ultimately, such assignments risk being perceived as little more than busywork. This is particularly problematic for assignments designed to teach students about library resources and services. When an assignment lacks a well-developed context, students view it as just something that needs to be completed for class rather than as something inherently useful.

Regardless, librarians are often caught in the middle. When students seek assistance, they may not have a copy of the assignment with them. Even if they do, it may be unclear what exactly the faculty member expects the students to do. This means the librarian must guess at what's expected. If the librarian underguesses, the student's grade may suffer. If the librarian overguesses, the student may end up doing more work than necessary. In both instances, the perception of that librarian's usefulness will be severely compromised. This perception is likely to carry over to the other librarians.

Suggestions

- Share an assignment's purpose/goals with other librarians most likely to assist students.
- Whenever possible, discuss specific goals and expectations with the faculty member *before* the assignment is distributed. If this isn't possible, try contacting the faculty member for clarification as soon as you encounter or otherwise learn of the problem. For additional discussion and suggestions about contacting and working with faculty members, please refer to chapter 2.

Unclear, Dated, or Inappropriate Terminology

Infrequent and less savvy users of the library may be unfamiliar with the terminology used in their particular library. For example, someone who assumes that all libraries use the Dewey Decimal Classification system will have difficulty finding the desired materials in a library that uses the Library of Congress system.

A growing problem is the wide variety and ever-changing nature of technology. New terms seem to emerge on a daily basis. Resources are updated regularly. As a result, a feature or resource that was formerly known by one name may now be referred to as something else. Similarly, new technologies are often confusing to those not familiar with them. For example, one person may use the term *online resource* to refer to a website, and another person may use the same term to refer to an electronic subscription resource.

Suggestions

- Clarify any ambiguous or potentially confusing terms with the faculty member.
- Avoid the use of jargon or library-specific terminology and names.

Missing Resources or Limited Resource Access

When a resource that students need to complete an assignment isn't available, their frustration rises dramatically. A printed resource may be unavailable because the item

isn't owned by the library

has been removed from the collection

is being processed (i.e., it's not yet available to the public)

is in the process of being reshelved

is housed in a restricted use/limited access area (e.g., archives, special collections)

has been stolen

is misshelved—accidentally or on purpose

has been discontinued or removed in favor of an electronic version

An electronic resource may be unavailable because

the resource or the technology used to access it is not functioning properly

the maximum number of simultaneous users has been reached

the link has been changed or moved

access is being attempted from an IP that falls outside the resource's allowable IP range

the student's account is somehow corrupted or incorrect, preventing authentication and access

the subscription has not yet been activated or properly linked

Suggestions

- When students are required to use a specific resource, place the item on reserve for the duration of the assignment to help ensure that it will be available to everyone.
- When a specified item is unavailable, clarify whether alternative versions or editions are acceptable. Similarly, if a specialized item isn't available (e.g., a pediatric nursing dictionary), determine if a related, more general resource is acceptable (e.g., a medical dictionary).

GENERAL ISSUES AND CONCERNS

In addition to the Big Three, there are a number of other general sorts of issues and concerns that may affect the overall effectiveness of an assignment. In the discussion below, those matters have been loosely grouped into administrative issues and perceptual issues.

Administrative Issues

Administrative issues are factors that affect the execution of an assignment. Whenever possible, faculty should strive to reduce or eliminate such factors to help ensure that assignments will produce the desired results.

Ever-Changing Resources

Ever-changing resources necessitate that assignments be updated frequently and regularly. Because resources, resource features, and resource access methods change all the time—particularly electronic ones—it is important to work with faculty to update assignments on a regular basis. Although the purpose of an assignment may remain the same, the way it is accomplished may need to be modified to reflect revised resources.

Suggestion

- Meet with faculty members prior to the start of a semester to discuss known changes and to suggest ways of addressing them. This can be done one-on-one or in groups as time and availability permit.

Inaccurate or Incomplete Citations

Inaccurate or incomplete citations make it difficult to find and use resources. Although this might seem obvious, syllabi and assignments with typographical errors and other incorrect information are not uncommon. Sometimes an item can be found using the incorrect information, but such success is more often a matter of sheer luck than of skill. Citations listing only partial information, such as an author and page number without a title, are equally troublesome.

Suggestion

- Be sure citations for required items correspond to the actual items.

Technology-Related Problems

Students may be unable or not know how to download or install required software. Because of viruses and other security threats, many campuses now deploy a variety of security measures on their networks. Similarly, to prevent students from accidentally erasing key programs and files, many systems are locked down so that students cannot access the hard drive. Although it should be possible to read or download data files and documents from a disc or web location, it may not be possible to install software, particularly if the software requires a reboot to complete the installation process. Many systems protect themselves by erasing anything new stored to the hard drive since the last restart. This includes software as well as any files a student may have been working on.

Suggestions

- Speak with faculty members about any software needs for their course.
- Recommend the use of standard software or whatever is standard for the institution.

Inaccessible Files

Desired files may be inaccessible. This problem has two levels. First, there are any number of things that can cause a file to become corrupted or otherwise unusable. The most common problem is that the storage device somehow becomes damaged (e.g., water spotted, scratched) or inaccessible (e.g., a student loses a memory device). However, projects involving multiple files, multiple file formats, or multiple students saving to or accessing their work from multiple locations or media can create file accessibility problems as well.

Second, students may wish to access a particular file at a later date only to find they can't. For example, they may be applying for a job or to a graduate school that requires them to submit a writing sample. Work stored and accessed via campus e-mail or a student's network account is particularly vulnerable in this respect. Such accounts are often purged at some point following the term in which a student graduates—and sometimes even the day after a student graduates or is no longer enrolled in courses for any reason.

A bigger problem, though, is that many students never make backup copies of their work. In fact, some students never save their work in the first place. Particularly for smaller assignments and assignments asking for student opinions (i.e., support not required), it is not uncommon for students to type and print without ever saving their work.

Suggestions

- As a rule of thumb, if it's important enough to type once, it's important enough to save twice. Students should be encouraged to make backup copies of their work. Ideally, backup copies should be made on two separate, independent storage media (e.g., hard drive and removable storage device).

■ Have students e-mail a copy of their file to themselves. Although not the best backup method, it at least ensures a second copy of their work will be available should they need it.

Incompatible Technologies

Technology used on campus or in a course may be incompatible with technology used at home. Technology is becoming increasingly seamless. However, differences in hardware or software can still cause problems. One of the most common problems in this respect is that computing technology and software may be from different generations. What the student has at home may be different from what's available on campus. In fact, what's available on campus may vary from building to building and from classroom to classroom.

Microsoft Office 2008 is a prime example. Files created in the that version are not directly compatible with earlier versions of Office. Either the new software must be purchased, a free compatibility pack must be downloaded, or users need to learn how to save files in a compatible format, typically an earlier version of the software. Translated, a student may create and save a file in the library and go to a classroom or home only to find that the file isn't accessible to work on or otherwise view.

Suggestions

■ Inform students of the software available in the library and of known compatibility issues they might encounter elsewhere on campus or when working from home.

■ Develop a handout describing known or suspected compatibility issues as well as suggested work-arounds to address those concerns.

■ Save files in a lowest-common-denominator format.

Expectations for Inappropriate or Unnecessary Printing

The rising costs of toner and paper have virtually eliminated the days of unlimited free printing in most libraries and on most campuses. Unfortunately, students have typically been the ones forced to absorb the costs. Faculty members need to be reminded that they are not the only professor requiring students to print out items. They also need to be sensitive to student finances. For example, although it may be desirable for each student in a class to have rough and final drafts of all the other students' term papers to review throughout the term, it may not be affordable for a growing number of students.

Various print systems are in place. Under the pay-as-you-go method, students pay for the number of pages they print using either cash or some sort of debit card, often money they've personally added to their student identification card. Under the print quota system, each student is allowed to print a specific number of pages during the academic year or term. When a student logs on to a campus computer, her account is activated, and each time she prints something, her account is automatically debited. Once she uses up her quota of printed pages, she must add money to her account out of her own pocket.

Regardless of the print system in place, the costs of printing something in black on standard white paper is usually significantly less than printing something in color or on nonstandard media (e.g., transparencies). In some courses, color printouts are more critical than others. Art history students who are studying paintings, for example, will probably use color printing more often than students in a philosophy course that focuses primarily on written texts.

Suggestions

- Determine what, if any, print quotas or other printing restrictions are in place — in the library and campuswide.
- Ensure that faculty are aware of alternative ways of making copies available to students (e.g., web pages, reserves).
- Encourage faculty to distinguish between necessary printing and recommended printing and to identify such priorities in their assignments.
- Alert students to possible ways they can save paper and printing costs (e.g., printing multiple PowerPoint slides per page).
- Identify other resources on campus that handle printing needs. Printing twenty copies of something at the campus print center may be cheaper than printing the same copies from a networked printer.
- Discourage any requirement for students to print something on nonstandard media unless such printing will not entail additional costs.
- Refer students to the campus print center or an appropriate department if the library cannot handle their print requests directly.

Perceptual Issues

Perceptual issues stem from preconceptions about libraries, librarians, or information that impede a student's ability to complete an assignment.

Misperception 1: Students Already Know How to Conduct Research/Use Information Effectively

When developing assignments, many faculty members operate under the misperception that students have already learned how to conduct research and use information effectively. This belief is related to the notion that all students come to class having already acquired the reading and writing skills they will need to complete their assignments. The resulting problems are exacerbated by the misperception that a single class session with a librarian will address all students' needs and concerns.

The sad reality is that many students do not have the skills they need to complete their assignments successfully and effectively. Some may not have been expected to use such skills in previous courses, and others may never have had the chance to master those skills in the first place. Table 3.1 presents some misperceptions and facts about students' research skills.

Suggestions

- Determine which skills students have prior to the distribution of an assignment. Even if a library instruction session can't be scheduled, at least you can be alerted to potential problems students may have completing their work.
- Meet with faculty members to review recent changes to resources, policies, and so on.

Misperception 2: A Single Library Instruction Session Is Sufficient

Most faculty will agree that it is valuable to have a librarian speak with their students about how to access and use library resources. However, students do not all have

TABLE 3.1   COMMON MISPERCEPTIONS ABOUT STUDENTS' RESEARCH SKILLS

MISPERCEPTION	FACT
Students have the necessary skills.	Many students have never needed or were never given the chance to acquire and apply the skills needed to use libraries and information effectively.
Students can transfer and adapt skills.	What students learned previously (e.g., MLA style) may not be directly transferable to the present class or assignment (e.g., expectation to use APA style).
Students know how and when to apply learned skills.	Students may have difficulty applying a particular concept or skill if the purpose, context, or expectations are not exactly the same as those in the situation in which they initially learned the concept or skill.
Students will remember what they've learned.	Because several school terms (or even years) may have passed since students acquired and used the expected skills, they may have forgotten what needs to be done and how to do it.
The skills that students need don't change.	Because resources change all the time and because resources vary from library to library, what students learned in the past may no longer be applicable or meaningful.
Whatever students have learned is adequate.	The skills and information students previously acquired may have been too specific, too general, or too philosophical to meet the needs of a particular assignment.

the same level of experience and skills with respect to technology and the use of information. Some students, for example, may already know how to use the library's catalog to find a book, whereas others may not even know what a catalog is, let alone how to use one.

This puts librarians in an extremely difficult position. Given that many faculty members are reluctant to schedule more than a single library instruction session, librarians are forced to decide whether to sacrifice depth for breadth or vice versa. That is, a conscious decision typically has to be made about whether to cover a few topics well or a lot of topics briefly. At the same time, a decision has to be made about whether to cover the basics or to focus on specific assignment-related concerns and resources. Either way, in a single session a librarian will rarely be able to cover everything students need to know and to address every issue they will encounter in completing their assignments.

Suggestions

- Faculty need to be reminded that, as with any skill, learning to use the library and information effectively requires both patience and practice. Whenever possible, a follow-up instruction session (or sessions) should be scheduled to address problems students encountered when completing their assignment or to discuss topics that weren't covered in previous sessions.
- If an additional session isn't possible, suggest a working day in the library or a computer lab on campus where you will be available to assist students one-on-one as they work on their projects.

Misperception 3: All Library Resources and Services Are Available to Everyone All the Time

Many libraries have unique local collections and resources that are invaluable to students. A university's newspaper collection on microfilm, for example, might prove especially useful to journalism majors studying language and how topics have been presented over time. The problem is that students may not be familiar with how to properly use the equipment needed to access this collection. A similar problem emerges with archives and other special collections that may be available a limited number of hours per day or by appointment only. This added hurdle can frustrate students and cause unanticipated delays in the completion of their assignments.

This is not just a problem with specialized collections. Even the newest electronic information resources may have restrictions on their use. Some information resources, for example, may be available only on campus or may require a password or help from a librarian. Downloading some sort of additional software (e.g., an applet) may also be required for full functionality. The licensing of some productivity software may impose further limitations. In some cases, only a specified number of users may be allowed to access the software at the same time. If that number is reached, an additional student will not be able to access the software until a current user exits. This can be particularly problematic if the permitted number of simultaneous users is low and the number of courses expecting students to use the software is high.

Suggestions

- Inform faculty members of any known restrictions — technical, mechanical, or administrative — involving the resources they wish their students to use.
- Suggest the institution or library explore ways of expanding access and use. Statistics documenting current use must often be gathered to support the case for expansion.

Misperception 4: Research Is Not Supposed to Be Fun or Easy

Although thorough research may not be fun or easy, it doesn't have to be unnecessarily difficult. For example, at first glance, requiring students to use microfilm to locate and photocopy the front page of a newspaper for the day of their birth may seem like a good way to introduce students to microfilm. However, with rare exceptions, many newspapers are now available electronically. Instead of learning when or why they should use microfilm (e.g., for much older items), students completing this assignment might become frustrated and conclude that using microfilm is just something they have to do to complete the assignment.

Suggestion

- Research doesn't have to be fun or easy, but research assignments should not be so difficult that students come to dread the research process.

Misperception 5: Librarians Have All the Answers

Although the thought that librarians have all the answers and can always be counted on for help is flattering, it is blatantly untrue. The amount and variety of information and information resources and services make it impossible for anyone to know everything. Like everyone, librarians have individual strengths and weaknesses. Most will be more knowledgeable in some areas than in others. Unfortunately, when students come to the library, the librarian who is available may not be particularly proficient in their area of need. Moreover, if assignments are poorly constructed or their expectations are unclear, every librarian's ability to help students is diminished.

Suggestions

- Librarians are only human and can't possibly know all there is to know or how to access every piece of information.
- Get copies of assignments before they are distributed, share them with the other librarians, and identify any potential problems.
- Work with students to the best of your ability and, when necessary, be willing to say you don't know how to help. However, if you do so, be sure to refer the students to someone who can indeed be of service.

Misperception 6: Students Don't Need Help in Figuring Out How to Use the Library

Faculty members often assume that students can figure out how to use the library on their own. In fact, however, many students have little experience using an academic library. Moreover, the Internet has made so many resources and services available from any computer that students may have seen no need to use the library. Even students who have used other libraries may not be prepared to use the campus library. Although many resources may be similar from one library to another, it is rare to find any two libraries with exactly the same resources, layout (e.g., locations), and methods of access. Similarly, just because students have some proficiency in using a computer does not necessarily mean that they can use those skills to locate and retrieve desired information.

Suggestions

- Remind faculty that what a student knows about using one library may or may not pertain to using another.
- Make sure that instructors realize that good computer skills do not necessarily translate into good research skills.

Misperception 7: Electronic Databases and Web Pages Are Navigated in the Same Way

Almost everyone nowadays is familiar with using browser buttons (e.g., Back) to navigate through information on the Web. Whether out of force of habit or lack of knowledge, many people use these same techniques when searching electronic information resources. However, within most electronic databases and indexes, use of browser buttons can cause any of a number of problems, such as incomplete or empty searches and printing errors. This can be especially problematic with proprietary browsers. Chapter 4 provides a more detailed discussion of issues surrounding the use of information technology.

Suggestion

- Students need to be told that once an electronic resource is accessed, browser buttons should be used only when the resource specifies their use or if there are no appropriate resource buttons available.

Misperception 8: Students Know All About Computers

Although it may be true that today's students generally have more computer skills than students in the past, many of those skills do not necessarily have practical value for completing assignments. Moreover, even students with good computer skills rarely have good information and research skills. Students often aren't aware of all the library's many and varied resources, how to access them, or how to search them effectively. Many students have difficulty determining what makes one source better or more appropriate than another.

Suggestions

- Work with faculty members to determine what skills are needed to complete a particular assignment and develop appropriate instruction, handouts, and so on.
- Create workshops, handouts, and other instructional methods for helping students adapt their technology skills to the research process.

Misperception 9: Everything Is Available Online Somewhere

When a faculty member tells students to go online to find what they need, the intended meaning isn't always clear. To most, this means going on the Internet, but some may understand that the reference is to electronic resources or services. Obviously, part of the problem is unclear terminology. But the fact that an Internet browser must be used at least to access the library's electronic databases only adds to the confusion. In addition, because most Internet searches produce some result, users assume that searching an electronic resource will produce results as well. However, the library may not have the most appropriate electronic resource for a course or an assignment, or students may not search the resource effectively.

Suggestions

- Ascertain exactly which electronic resources a faculty member expects students to use. Many instructors discourage or prohibit the use of the Internet.
- Work with faculty and departments to ensure the library has appropriate resources—printed and electronic.

Misperception 10: Information Found on the Web Is Inevitably Bad

The misperception that information found on the Internet is unreliable is based on the assumption that books, articles, and other forms of printed information are superior to web sources. Admittedly, there are countless questionable sites on the Internet. Likewise, the majority of information is still produced in printed form. However, as with printed resources, there are both good and bad sources of information on the Web. It's up to information consumers to decide which sources best meet their needs. In fact, a growing number of libraries actually encourage use of the Web for information and resources. This is often prompted by budgetary constraints (i.e., libraries can't buy everything) as well as by the sheer quantity and variety of information available via the Internet.

Suggestions

- The best research is based on a variety of sources. Be sure faculty members are aware of resource strengths and weaknesses in terms of availability, content, focus, and the like.
- Create an online list of quality websites (and other resources) that students might find useful in completing a specific assignment. Be warned, though. Depending on the specificity required by the assignment, such lists can quickly become quite lengthy. Like the assignments they support, such lists require frequent and regular monitoring and updating regardless of their size.

FOUR USING INFORMATION TECHNOLOGY

DESCRIPTION

It is impossible for students to complete an assignment without using some sort of information technology. However, the term *information technology* means different things to different people. When asked, most people associate this term with resources used to access and retrieve information, such as the library's catalog and electronic databases. In this context, printed journals, maps, and any other material that provides information could be considered information technology as well.

But changes in society and in higher education combined with the explosion of information necessitate expanding to a much broader, more comprehensive definition of *information technology*. It is this evolved definition that provides the context for this chapter. This definition would include any technology used to access, retrieve, manage, or manipulate information in an ethical and legal manner. In addition to databases and indexes, this more inclusive definition would incorporate software such as that used for creating and managing bibliographies (e.g., RefWorks, EndNote) as well as word processing, spreadsheet, and presentation software (e.g., PowerPoint), among others. This broader definition would also include hardware that enables individuals to digitize analog information (e.g., VHS-to-digital converters).

Why is an evolved definition needed? The traditional definition falls short in two important ways. First, there is a growing emphasis on accountability in higher education. Colleges and universities are expected to produce graduates who can succeed in today's knowledge society. Second, because they provide a framework for assessing outcomes (i.e., accountability), expectations for information literacy are increasingly being incorporated into assignments, courses, and both curriculum and accreditation standards.

As discussed in chapter 1, the Association of College and Research Libraries has published standards for information literacy in higher education that address competency in the following areas:

1. Defining research needs

2. Accessing information

3. Locating relevant information

4. Critically evaluating information

5. Employing ethical principles

The traditional interpretation of the term *information technology* tends to focus only on the first two or three IL standards. In addition, it concentrates almost exclusively on printed and textual forms of information even though information now exists and is used in many formats and contexts. Video and audio files, for example, are increasingly being incorporated into presentations. In the past, giving a presentation that included video and audio typically involved hauling and setting up various pieces of equipment (e.g., TVs, VCRs) at the presentation location. It was such a cumbersome process that presenters often overlooked nontextual information or used it sparingly. Today, electronic files make it easier to include such information in presentations.

THE NEED

Technology and course assignments are now inextricably linked. In the bygone print world, assignments were pretty straightforward: students needed to know how to read, write, and (maybe) type. If the results were to be presented to a group, they were usually presented orally and, therefore, virtually any venue was adequate. Technology, if any, may have consisted of a microphone, screen, and slide projector or TV/VCR unit.

Today, though, the assignment process is radically different. From the conducting of research to the presentation of findings, students must cope with issues related to information technology that are as broad and as plentiful as the technologies themselves. In short, although technology has greatly facilitated the use of information, it has also created a whole new group of problems. Because the vast and ever-changing array of technologies makes it is impossible to discuss every possible problem students might encounter, this chapter necessarily focuses on some of the more universal issues.

THE CHALLENGES

In addition to considering the general technology-related issues outlined below, librarians need to ascertain the unique technology challenges faced by students at their institution. They should also do all they can to make faculty aware of the challenges posed by information technology and how they affect students' completion of assignments.

Changes to Resources or Resource Access

As previously discussed, the tools, services, and resources students will use to complete assignments will vary from library to library and over time. As a result, what students have learned in the past may not be applicable to their present needs or circumstances. Adding to the problem is the fact that resources change all the time. Most libraries try to schedule changes and updates during downtime (e.g., during semester breaks). But, many times, updates and other changes are made without notice and are beyond the library's control. The five most common changes to resource technologies are changes in name, changes in location, addition of new resources, removal of old resources, and changes in interface.

Changes in Name

Although it doesn't happen very often, resource names do change. Most of the time, the vendor initiates this sort of change. For example, new content, new features, and changes in coverage may prompt a vendor to rename a resource to reflect the revisions and to differentiate the revised version from the old one. However, it is not unheard of for libraries to change resources' names. This is often done in order to brand the resource to reflect local constituents or curricular concerns. The addition of *PITT* to the name of the University of Pittsburgh's catalog to form PITTCat is a good example.

A more common problem is the confusion that may arise when a change is made to the name of the link from which a resource can be accessed. A library may, for example, decide to change from the more general Databases to the more specific Finding Articles even though both links point to the library's list of electronic databases for finding articles.

Changes in Location

The location of resources may change as well. Books, for example, are often moved as new items are added and old items are removed from the collection. Although the call number remains the same, the physical location of the books may change. For electronic resources, it's no different. As an ever-growing number of resources become available via the Internet, more and more links to them are being embedded in web pages. But as web designers and others manipulate the content of web pages, what once was linked in one place may be moved and linked somewhere else. In addition, some resources are still loaded and are only available locally. Good examples are CDs, DVDs, and client-based applications. In such cases, not just the link to the resource but also the entire machine on which the resource is loaded may change locations.

Addition of New Resources

Libraries typically offer a wide array of resources—both printed and electronic. However, the number that actually gets used can often be disappointingly limited. This may be just as attributable to poor publicity about the resources as it is to researchers' tendencies to use what they're used to using. For example, students typically become familiar with a handful of electronic resources—typically those most relevant to their major or available through a particular vendor. As a result, when new resources are added, it's not surprising that they often get overlooked. For example, students may be used to searching EBSCOHost resources and be completely unaware that non-EBSCOHost resources even exist, much less that new ones have been added. An even more common problem affects the lists of resources that many libraries maintain. If a list contains more than a handful of resources, new additions are less likely to be seen or noticed.

Removal of Old Resources

Just as print resources may be removed, access to electronic resources may be discontinued for any of a number of reasons (e.g., limited use, budget cutbacks). As a result, students trying to access a resource with which they're familiar may not be able to find it. In many cases, they assume that the link to their desired resource has merely been changed or moved. Until they speak with a librarian, they often don't consider that access to the resource is no longer possible.

Changes in Interface

Perhaps the most confounding type of change is that involving the interface of a familiar resource. Librarians spend a good deal of time assisting and instructing students in how to use resources effectively. Thus, when a vendor adds new features or functionality to a resource, problems may well arise. For example, a library may have a database that enables users to limit results to peer-reviewed journals versus magazines. Then, in an upgrade, the vendor decides to provide a new limit for scholarly publications. As a result of the change, students needing to search for articles from academic journals may not realize that they need to limit their searching to peer-reviewed or to scholarly publications. Librarians will then have to spend time assisting and reeducating countless users about the relation of scholarly and peer-reviewed publications: Is one a subset of the other, or are they two separate types of periodicals?

Suggestions

- Advise faculty members of resource changes regularly and as soon as possible. Participating in faculty in-service and other orientation activities at the start of each semester is a good way to do so.
- Use any and all available means to alert users to resource changes. Among the possible channels of communication are the library or campus news services (e.g., newspaper, newsletter, radio), blogs, a What's New? link off the library's home page, signage, and pop-up windows on log-in.

- Maintain an updated list of access codes, procedures, and licensing restrictions as well as common access problems (and solutions) that you can share with faculty members and their students.
- To help improve users' ability to transfer knowledge across resources, encourage instruction that focuses on broad concepts rather than on specific keystrokes or features. For example, even though two indexes may be referring to the same thing, one may use the term *peer reviewed* to describe academic journals, whereas another might use the term *academic* or *scholarly*. Rather than focusing on the name of the feature and telling students to look for the "peer reviewed" search option, emphasize that most resources enable individuals to narrow their searches to professional-level content—regardless of what the search feature is called.

Connectivity Issues

Although the use of dial-up access to the Internet is decreasing, in some areas it is still the only connection option. The relative slowness of dial-up services can result in a number of problems related to library resources. Most resources, for example, have a time-out feature. If activity doesn't occur or an action is not completed within a set period of time, the resource essentially shuts down. Among other things, this can result in the loss of data, incomplete searches, and, in many cases, the need to reconnect to the resource and start over.

Timing out may also cause difficulties when students try to access or download files. For example, although less of a problem than in the past, large PDF files may be hard to download using dial-up access. In a best-case scenario, a large file will not download completely before a time-out occurs, and users will have to attempt to download the file again. However, in many instances, a computer may freeze, forcing the user to restart—the resource, the Internet session, or even the entire system.

Suggestions

- Talk with the person responsible for administering the resource and make the default time-out value larger.
- Provide a list of dial-up-friendly suggestions to assist off-site users.
- Create persistent links to frequently accessed searches and sources of information. This feature allows instructors to embed a link on a web page. Students can then quickly access the link to an article rather than having to access a resource and conduct an entire search.

Access Issues

Even when connections are good, there are still a number of general access issues students may encounter. For example, students may have difficulty accessing resources remotely. Some may not know the procedure for doing so or try to use an incorrect procedure. Others may find that needed resources require the user to be on campus or even in the library. This is particularly problematic for students in online courses who may not have access to the physical campus.

Licensing or network restrictions may also affect a user's ability to access a resource. Some licensing, for example, may prohibit a resource's use by alumni, townspeople, and others not directly affiliated with the institution. Local network restrictions may preclude certain individuals from accessing particular technologies or even from getting onto a computer in the first place. For example, a university might lock a user account that hasn't been used in more than thirty days. As a result, students completing an internship or studying abroad may find their accounts frozen even though they are clearly still students.

A more common problem is user limits. These may be imposed by the institution, but, more often than not, they are imposed by the vendor. Here, a resource is licensed for a set number of concurrent users. If that number of users is currently accessing the resource, additional individuals wishing to use the resource need to try again later. Limits are especially frustrating for students when a resource's maximum number of users is small and its use is required for a course they are taking. If a resource's limit is fifty users, for example, and several hundred students are required to use it, some individuals may not be able to access the resource at their desired time.

Suggestions

- Determine which courses will be using resources with user limits and either increase the number of possible concurrent users or alert faculty that there may be access issues, particularly if multiple classes will need to use the resource during the same portion of the term.
- Identify the common reasons an individual might have difficulty accessing resources and alert faculty members to them so that the matter can be addressed accordingly.

Ineffective, Inefficient, or Inappropriate Search Strategies

Students may encounter many pitfalls when they try to conduct research. Sometimes students don't find what they're seeking because they're not sure what they want or need to find. More often than not, though, it is their search strategy that is at fault. Five of the most common problems associated with student search strategies are outlined below. Librarians should strongly encourage instructors to schedule an instructional presentation during which means of overcoming these pitfalls can be discussed.

Inappropriate Topics

One of the biggest challenges student researchers face is developing a researchable topic. Many have good ideas or an interest in a particular topic they wish to explore. The difficulty comes in transforming that topic into one that's researchable. In many cases, students begin with a topic that is too broad or too narrow. In other instances, the library may not have adequate resources for the topic a student is trying to research. Still other students don't understand that evolving a topic doesn't necessarily mean changing it. Students need to understand that as they learn more about a topic, they are likely to find a new aspect or perspective they wish to explore.

Suggestions

- Emphasize the importance of developing a topic before beginning the search for information.
- Suggest ways of focusing a topic until it becomes researchable and meets assignment requirements.

Inappropriate Resources

Students often have trouble identifying which resource to use when conducting their research. It may be that they don't know which resource is the most relevant. They may be overwhelmed by the number of choices. Or they may not be able to determine the advantages of using one resource over another. When students aren't finding relevant material, they need to be made aware that it may be because the resource they're using isn't the most appropriate one or does not sufficiently index material on their topic. At the same time, students also need to be reminded it is unlikely—particularly for term papers and other more demanding research projects—that a single resource will produce all of the necessary (or available) information to complete their assignment.

Suggestions

- Direct students to resources most likely to index material on their topic.
- Work with students to explore their topics from different perspectives. The death penalty, for example, could as easily be explored from a criminal justice perspective as from a sociological one.
- Suggest students search additional resources to obtain desired information.

Inappropriate Search Terms

One of the key research challenges faced by many students is converting their topic into suitable search terms. They may have a few ideas to start with but can quickly become frustrated if those terms don't produce the desired results. Related terms and concepts are often overlooked. At that point, it is not uncommon to find students wagging the dog. That is, students change their topic based on the results of their research rather than letting their topic guide them through the research process.

Suggestions

- Work with students to identify alternative terms and concepts related to their topic. For example, searches for *adolescents, teens, teen agers, teenagers, young adults,* and *minors* will all produce similar yet differing results.

- Determine if search terms have alternative spellings (e.g., *Brazil* and *Brasil*).
- Ask students if historical, geographical, or other factors might affect their search terms. The terms *Negroes, Blacks,* and *African Americans,* for example, all refer to the same racial group but were used in different time periods.
- Always check search terms for spelling and typing errors.
- Encourage students to find additional search terms by consulting a dictionary, a thesaurus, or the index or subject headings of a topic-related resource.

Inappropriate Strategy

Even when students have a researchable topic, pick the right resource, and have a good set of search terms, they may still not be employing the most appropriate search strategy. Most students are familiar with the Internet, which basically generates results by matching text entered into a search engine. Many students, though, are unfamiliar with searching databases and electronic indexes for information. They assume that searching them is no different from searching the Internet. Even students who are aware of databases and electronic indexes may not know the correct ways to use features such as searching by subject and limiting results to a given range of dates. The potential confusion is compounded by the fact that features and strategies that work in one resource may not be available or work the same way in another resource.

Suggestions

- Work with faculty and students to ensure they know how to use a desired resource.
- Teach how databases and indexes use fields and limits to facilitate searching.
- Suggest that students do a basic search to get started and then use advanced search options to focus searches.

Meta-searching

Meta-searching is an increasingly common strategy used by many students. It essentially involves searching multiple resources simultaneously. With database searches, users might choose resources from an alphabetical list or from a list of resources affiliated with a given topic or discipline. On the Web, meta-searching employs multiple search engines on a single search. Meta-searching is popular because it eliminates the need to do the same searches on multiple resources. Meta-searching is currently done by keyword. Consequently, result sets tend to be rather large and unfocused, which makes meta-searching an excellent tool for browsing and generating general information on a given topic. At the same time, however, because the benefits of the unique, advanced search features of each resource are compromised or unavailable during a meta-search, it is usually difficult to refine a search beyond common, basic limits or fields (e.g., date). Researchers wishing to do more specific, focused searching must then access the appropriate resources individually.

Suggestions

- Help students realize that conducting a specific, sophisticated search on one resource may produce better results (and ultimately be less time-consuming) than using keywords to do a cursory search of multiple resources.
- Suggest meta-searching for browsing and generating ideas but not for conducting research.

Inability to Use Hardware or Software

Whether or not instructors assume that students already have the necessary technical and research skills, the question remains of how students who lack such skills can acquire them. For example, on the surface, having students in a marketing course produce their own television advertisements seems like an appropriate assignment. However, some students, even if they have great ideas, may have no notion of how to use a digital video recorder and video editing software to convert their visions into concrete form. It is unrealistic to expect that everyone has expertise in using a given piece of hardware or software package—no matter how commonplace or ubiquitous that technology is or seems to be.

Suggestions

- Develop a list of campus workshops and other educational opportunities where students can learn how to use various pieces of hardware and software.
- Create instruction geared to a specific course or assignment.

Hardware and Software Incompatibility

Although software and hardware are increasingly seamless, compatibility issues have not disappeared entirely. The computer a student works on at home may be more (or less) sophisticated than the ones used on campus. Even on campus, the software and hardware available on one machine may not be available on another. File types readable on one system may be unreadable or display differently on another. Similarly, older editions of software may not open or properly display files created in more recent versions of the same software.

Suggestion

- Develop and distribute a list of known and potential compatibility issues students might encounter.

Unavailable Technology

Obviously, if a technology isn't available, students can't use it to complete their work. For example, though making color printouts or photocopies might be desirable, the technology may not be available for students to do so. If it is, it may involve an extra fee. It may also necessitate that students make special accommodations to use the technology. For example, maybe the campus copy center is only open certain hours, or perhaps the use of a color printer requires the assistance of a staff member.

Suggestions

- At the start of every term, inform faculty about which technologies and services are no longer available or have undergone changes.
- When a technology is required but is unavailable, work with faculty members to determine alternative technologies that are acceptable.

Getting Online Is Not Good Enough

The Internet is increasingly becoming students' first (and often only) stop in the research process. Unfortunately, some faculty members don't expect anything more and, therefore, reinforce students' use of the Internet as their only research tool. The growing number of sites purporting to provide full-text articles only adds to the problem. In many cases, they don't provide content from professional journals. If they do, they often charge a fee for access when the same material may be available for free via the library's databases. Either way, poor search strategies, the inability to do more than keyword searching, and the preponderance of dated, misleading, or even inaccurate information often renders the quality of many Internet search results dubious at best. In turn, that diminishes the overall quality of the finished product and often causes it to fall short of what was intended.

Suggestions

- To help improve the quality of the source material students use, strongly advocate that faculty members prohibit Internet research and require the use of library resources and services to locate articles and other sources of information.
- Explain the advantages and disadvantages of using the Internet to find information.
- Instruct students how to evaluate the relevance and accuracy of information they find.

FIVE WRITING-FROM-SOURCES AND ESSAY ASSIGNMENTS

DESCRIPTION

Writing-from-sources and essay assignments are among the most common types of library assignments. Both can serve as introductions to specific library resources and are often used as a means of teaching students the basic elements of researching, organizing, and presenting their thoughts and ideas. As such, they may be either stand-alone assignments or serve as precursors to larger projects.

When an assignment calls for writing from sources, the nature of the finished product can be just about anything. Some may require students to examine abstracts, whereas others want students to use a particular resource. All such assignments involve learning about some aspect of the library's organization (e.g., call numbers) or require students to use some sort of source material or resource.

Essays are short works of prose that discuss one topic or idea. An essay is essentially an attempt to put one's thoughts into words and stems from the French infinitive *essayer*, meaning "to try." Essays often focus on students' writing as much as on the process used to complete the assignment. As with all assignments, expectations in terms of length, formatting, source material, and other considerations will vary. Still, virtually all essays require students to conduct some rudimentary research. For example, students might be required to locate and cite five sources of information that support a particular position on an issue.

The most basic form of essay follows a standard five-paragraph format as described in table 5.1. Many advocate using the five-paragraph format as a way of helping students organize and present their thoughts. Others argue, though, that such a format is restrictive and overly simplistic. The essay format used will ultimately be as reflective of the type of essay as it is of the course, the discipline, and the faculty member's specific goals for the assignment.

TIME FRAME

The time frame for completing an essay or writing-from-sources assignment will typically vary from a few days to a few weeks. Length requirements, the number of sources to be cited, and the complexity of formatting (e.g., use of citations) are but a few of the factors that will affect how much time is allotted.

INTENDED PURPOSES

The purpose of writing-from-sources and essay assignments is typically dependent upon the assignment itself. Four of the most common reasons behind writing-from-sources and essay assignments include expectations that the student will learn about

1. *Organizing and presenting ideas.* As noted above, the five-paragraph format of the basic essay serves as a good introduction to organizing and presenting ideas. In addition, it serves its purpose without being overly time-consuming or difficult. Such essays can stand on their own or set the stage for additional essays or for larger, term projects (see chapter 6). When the use of source material is required, students are forced to learn how to read and digest what they've read in order to successfully complete the assignment.

2. *A particular topic or issue.* Some writing assignments focus on developing students' knowledge of and familiarity with a topic or an issue. The information gathered is inherently useful but may also be used to build a foundation for discussion and understanding of subsequent topics or issues.

3. *The research process.* Although on a much smaller, more focused scale, essays mirror many of the elements of larger research projects (e.g., using secondary sources, citing sources). For this reason, they are often assigned as a way of introducing students to the research process.

TABLE 5.1   OVERVIEW OF STANDARD FIVE-PARAGRAPH ESSAY

PARAGRAPH(S)	HEADING	DESCRIPTION
1	Introduction	Main idea/thesis statement presented
2–4	Content	Three paragraphs, each of which provides evidence in support of the thesis statement
5	Conclusion	Restatement of the thesis statement and support

4. *The library.* Some essays are assigned as a way of introducing students to library resources and services. For example, students may be required to write an essay using information found in a subject dictionary and a book of their choice. This forces students to find specific items and access the information they contain.

WHAT *NOT* TO DO

The examples in this section come from actual assignments shared with me while compiling information for this book and demonstrate some of the common problems associated with writing-from-sources and essay assignments. Although edited for length, the excerpts are quoted verbatim, and every attempt was made to preserve the flavor and context of the original. The first example is extracted from a writing-from-sources assignment that focuses on content. The second is also from a writing-from-sources assignment but requires the use of a specific resource. The final example represents a typical essay assignment.

Example 1: Content-Based Writing from Sources

The content-based writing-from-sources assignment below was titled "Assignment #1: Two Abstracts" and was due in late September. The boldface appears in the original.

> For this assignment, you need to find two empirical research studies from professional journals . . . which examine the effectiveness of specific treatment approaches for particular disorders . . . **one research article must be found in a journal available in the library.** You must go to the library and copy the abstract of the article. **(Do not use an online full text source for this article.)**

Problems

Questionable relevance. The purpose of this assignment seems to be to teach students the value of printed resources. Given that the majority of information has been and continues to be produced in printed format, requiring students to become familiar with the use of printed resources seems like a worthwhile exercise. However, with more and more journals being made available electronically and as retrospective coverage continues to expand, the value of locating the actual, original printed version of a journal article is becoming increasingly dubious. Moreover, many electronic resources provide access to the full text of journals to which the library has never subscribed. Therefore, particularly at smaller libraries with limited journal collections, requiring students to focus on printed versions may impose unnecessary and even inappropriate limitations on their research.

Limited availability of printed journals. With the ever-growing online availability of full-text journals, many libraries are canceling their printed journal subscriptions in favor of the electronic versions. In turn, many are also removing their printed copies to make room for other resources, study areas, and so on. As a result, at many libraries, it is becoming increasingly difficult (if not impossible) to locate printed versions of journals and articles. Even if printed versions do exist, the desired issues or pages may be missing or damaged, necessitating that the student conduct additional searches.

Implied knowledge and availability of appropriate search tools and strategies. Although it is becoming increasingly uncommon, some libraries still do not have their entire printed collection linked to their electronic indexes and search tools. In such cases, students may not be able to limit their search to the printed collection. In addition, they may need to use printed indexes and abstracts to find older articles. Those resources are virtually unknown to most students and are seen as incredibly cumbersome and tedious to use. Even if the collections are linked, students may not know how to use their search results to locate the desired printed journal.

Revised Example 1

Note that the revised example indicates that some sort of library instruction has been provided to students. Although they may still have trouble choosing the best resource for their topic and developing an effective search strategy, they have at least been exposed to basic resources and search strategies in preparation for completing the assignment. As the focus of this assignment is on finding relevant source material, the original version's prohibition of using electronic versions has also been altered to focus on the availability (i.e., not the media) of both the journal and the article.

> Using the techniques outlined in class, find two empirical research studies from professional, scholarly journals that examine the effectiveness of specific treatments for the disorder you've selected. For each resource, please provide the following information:
> 1. Identify the name of the resource you used to find each article.
> 2. Write a complete citation for each article, including the abstract.
> 3. Indicate whether each article is available in printed and/or electronic format. If an article is not available in either format, complete—*but do NOT submit*—an interlibrary loan (ILL) form and turn it in with your assignment.
> 4. Indicate whether the library has printed and/or electronic access to each journal. If so, list the volumes, issues, and dates for each format.

Example 2: Resource-Based Writing from Sources

A resource-based assignment is often distributed to first-year students as a rudimentary way of familiarizing them with how to use library resources and services. Content still plays a role, but in contrast to the example above, greater emphasis is placed on having students gain experience in using a specific library resource. Although the sample assignment pertains to microfilm, the related problems are not uncommon to other library resources.

Use the library's microfilm collection to locate the front page of the *New York Times* for your date of birth. Copy the page. Then, using the articles which appear on the front page, write a 2- to 3-page paper summarizing two of the things that were happening on that day.

Problems

Burden on library staff. Assignments involving microfilm typically require countless hours of personal assistance. First and foremost, microfilm is a technology unfamiliar to most students. They need to be taught how to find the items they seek and then how to use the equipment to access the information. The learning curve is steepened by the fact that the library may have several different types of machines, each with unique features. For example, some machines may only be able to read microfilm, whereas others may be able to both read microfilm and print its content. In addition, in many libraries, microfilm equipment may be old and subject to malfunction. Coin and paper jams as well as misfed reels are just a few of the problems students will commonly experience.

Potential lack of resource relevance. Arguably, there is a lot of worthwhile information stored on microfilm. In some instances, the information isn't available anywhere else. For some majors (e.g., history, journalism), microfilm can be a valuable learning tool. And yet, after completing the assignment, many students will never use this resource again. Too, much of what the assignment asks students to find is available much more readily via electronic means. Consequently, students often view this sort of assignment as little more than busywork. Rather than discovering when and why microfilm is valuable, they learn that it is an arcane, problematic, and frustrating technology.

Equipment-related issues. Many libraries have a very limited number of microfilm machines. Because of this and the expense incurred if the machines are broken, many microfilm areas have use restrictions. This can be problematic when all students from a single class, let alone students from multiple classes, are working on the assignment at the same time. Adding to this problem is the likelihood of misshelved or mislaid reels and the possibility that reels may rip (i.e., due to heavy use), making them unavailable for use. Beyond that, printing and other equipment-related problems may crop up. To print an entire front page of a newspaper, for example, requires oversized paper. Given that such paper may not be available, students will be forced to reduce the page to fit on a standard sheet of paper, resulting in printouts with small, unreadable type, or they will need to print multiple 8½-by-11-inch sheets and piece them together.

Revised Example 2

For any of a number of reasons, faculty members are sometimes unwilling to change the substance of their assignments. However, most are open to changing the wording if it results in an improved finished product. In the case of this sample assignment, the professor insisted that his students experience the use of microfilm, so the instruction librarian had to be content with his acceptance of a few subtle changes in wording. Although the changes do not address all of the possible problems, they at least reinforce the role microfilmed resources can play in the research process.

> Electronic full-text articles provide the same content as the original printed versions, but they don't provide the same context. Seeing the entire publication enables you to develop a sense of what else was happening at the time, which can help you to better understand the topic you're researching. Microfilm is one of the technologies libraries have available to help you to do this.
>
> To familiarize yourself with the use of microfilmed materials, select a date before 1950 that has historical significance or is important to you personally (e.g., a grandparent's birthday). Locate the front page of the *New York Times* for that day and write down the main headline as well as two other headlines. Then write a 2- to 3-page paper summarizing two of the things that were happening on that day.

Example 3: Essays Based on Sources

This example comes from an English 101 course, typically taken by undergraduates during their first term in college. The assignment was labeled "Argument Essay."

> Write a five-page paper that takes a position on one side of one of the topics below; your purpose is to take a stand on an issue and argue persuasively in support of it . . . Use the "peer-reviewed" option to limit searches . . . Your sources must come from reputable outlets. You *may not* use electronic sources that are not available through the library's database.

Problems

Appropriateness of peer-reviewed resources. The value of peer-reviewed, scholarly sources should not be minimized. And yet, for an introductory English course, restricting students to peer-reviewed resources may have the exact opposite effect of what was intended. This requirement gives the misleading impression that good information *only* appears in peer-reviewed publications. Clearly this is not true. An arguably bigger problem rests in the fact that, for numerous reasons (e.g., lack of subject knowledge, inability to interpret statistics), many first-year students may not yet be able to successfully read and digest a peer-reviewed article. That may turn them off and lead them to avoid such articles in the future in favor of more readable journals and articles.

Implications of requiring peer-reviewed sources. Another problem stems from the assignment's implication that the professor is familiar with all publications and all disciplines. Admittedly, students should be weaned from using sources like *People* magazine and *Reader's Digest* to complete college-level assignments, especially in upper-level courses. And yet, requiring students to use only peer-reviewed sources implies, among other things, that the professor is able to discern whether or not a given source is peer reviewed (presumably just by looking at the title) and whether or not the information a student includes in this sort of assignment is accurate.

Unclear wording/terminology. The last sentence in the example is confusing on a couple of levels. First, *electronic sources* is a very broad term. Given the last part of the sentence, the term presumably refers to library databases. And yet, if the sentence isn't read carefully, it could easily be misinterpreted to mean websites. Potentially even more problematic is the use of the singular term *database*. At the time, the library in question subscribed to more than a hundred electronic databases and indexes. Thus, it is unclear whether the faculty member is expecting students to use a single database or thinks that all databases are available via one single point of access. Either way, the wording is ambiguous and suggests there is only one resource that will provide good information.

Revised Example 3

The goal of the third sample assignment seems to be to get students to use peer-reviewed publications. However, as originally written the assignment suggests that only peer-reviewed publications are reputable. Obviously, there are many publications that provide excellent information (e.g., *National Geographic*) but are not peer reviewed. Thus, a key way to improve the assignment is by clarifying what is meant by "reputable outlets" and whether the only reputable outlets are peer-reviewed publications. The revision makes it clear that both peer-reviewed and non-peer-reviewed publications may be used to complete the assignment.

> Write a five-page paper that takes a position on one side of one of the topics below. Your purpose is to take a stand on an issue and argue persuasively in support of or in opposition to it. Using the library's databases and indexes, generate a list of five relevant articles from credible sources that support your argument and use three of them to write your essay. At least one of your five sources should be from a scholarly, peer-reviewed journal. Provide complete citations for all five sources at the end of your essay. Be sure to indicate the peer-reviewed source or sources and which three sources you actually used.

ISSUES/CONCERNS
Type of Essay Is Unclear or Not Identified

Assignments do not always specify which type of essay students are expected to write. Often students are merely told to write a five-page paper on a topic of their choosing. Although giving students such breadth may seems like a good thing, it can actually cause a lot of anxiety. Some students, when faced with so many options, may not know where to begin. Others, even if they have a sense of what they'd like to write about, may be unaware of or overlook the importance of choosing a particular type of essay to write before they begin their research. Table 5.2 provides an overview of six common types of essays that students are commonly asked to write. In order to develop an effective search strategy, it is essential that students first determine the type of essay they plan to write.

Suggestion

- Encourage faculty to review the types of essays in class and to make sure that each assignment specifies the type of essay students are to write.

Students Have Difficulties Selecting a Researchable Topic

Assuming students know which type of essay they're writing, their next biggest problem is selecting and articulating a topic that is researchable. Problems in this respect typically take three forms: topics that are too narrow or too broad, topics for which resources are too limited, and topics that lack a specified perspective.

TABLE 5.2   SIX COMMON TYPES OF ESSAYS

ESSAY TYPE	PRIMARY INTENT/PURPOSE	EXAMPLE
Argumentative/ persuasive	Persuade readers to adopt a point of view through the use of statistics, expert opinion, and other evidence	Solar energy is a viable alternative to fossil fuels.
Compare/contrast	Show similarities and/or differences between two topics or ideas	How do the views of Republicans and Democrats differ?
Critical/evaluative	Analyze another's work (e.g., book, movie) or elements of a work	How did metaphor contribute to the success of the movie *Citizen Kane*?
Definition	Define or explain a specific term or set of related concepts	What is love?
Informational/ descriptive	Describe what something is or how it happened	What events led to the start of World War I?
Process	Describe how something is done	How does one change a tire?

Topics Are Too Narrow or Too Broad

Perhaps the most common topic-related problem students have is selecting one that is too broad or too narrow. An essay on the revolution, for example, is much too broad and ambiguous. Conversely, an essay on the impact of a particular teaching style on female third-graders of Hispanic single-parent families at Grover Cleveland Elementary School in Detroit, Michigan, is too narrow. In the first case, the student is likely to find too much information, and in the second case the student will find too little.

Suggestion

- Tell instructors about the common problems students have in narrowing and broadening assignment topics and how such difficulties can be avoided.

Topics Are Not Supported by Adequate Resources

Some topics may not be researchable because the library doesn't have suitable resources. Most academic libraries focus on collecting resources that support the various courses and disciplines of the institution. As a result, for example, the library is likely to have a very limited collection of books and periodicals on cooking unless a course or program on cooking is offered. A public library may be more likely to have sources on this particular topic.

Suggestions

- Work with faculty members to review students' topics before they begin the assignment to identify potential topics with limited resources and decide how such topics can be modified or if they should be eliminated.
- Work with faculty members to develop and distribute a list of suggested resources based on workable student topics.

Topics Lack a Specified Perspective

In developing their topics, students may know which perspective they'll be writing from but neglect to incorporate it into their search strategy. For example, when writing an essay on school dress codes, a student will need to identify whether he'll be writing from the perspective of a teacher, parent, administrator, or student. Students who don't clearly articulate the perspective they'll be using may find information on their topic but not necessarily the information they seek.

Suggestion

- Encourage faculty members to emphasize the importance of a specified perspective when discussing topic selection with their classes.

Assigned Topics May Present Difficulties

One of the biggest problems with assigning topics to write about is that students may have little to no interest in the topics they've been assigned. This is particularly true of professors' pet topics and topics that have little to do with the course or a student's major field of study. In response, students are more likely to do the minimal amount of work necessary to complete the assignment. Although there is no guarantee that students who choose their own topics will go the extra mile, they will at least be interested in their topic and may do more and better work as a result.

Topics Aren't Assigned Methodically

Another problem pertains to how the topics are assigned. Whether instructors assign topics arbitrarily or try to match topics to students' specific needs or interests, the outcome can be problematic. When professors assign topics arbitrarily, for example, they risk assigning a complex topic to a student who may already be having difficulty with the course. Conversely, if they try to match each student with an appropriate topic, they risk claims of favoritism or vindictiveness.

Suggestions

- Work with faculty members to develop lists of topics related to the major disciplines of students in their classes.
- Suggest faculty members hold a lottery to determine the order in which students will select assigned topics.

Assigned Topics Serve Faculty Members' Purposes

Still, many faculty members feel the advantages to themselves far outweigh the disadvantages to students and assign topics accordingly. A few of the many reasons faculty members assign topics rather than allowing students to select their own are outlined below.

Lack of familiarity with students' chosen topics. When students choose their own topics, the faculty member may have little or no knowledge of the subject matter. In such cases, grading the final product becomes problematic as there is no easy way of determining the veracity of the information presented.

The need for variety. Reading more than a handful of papers on the same topic can become tedious very quickly on a number of levels. By assigning a range of topics, the instructor ensures variety.

Concerns about plagiarism. By assigning topics, faculty members have greater control over the final product. This makes it much easier to check for and to spot plagiarism. Similarly, even though plagiarism is still a possibility, assigning topics helps to reduce the risk because students won't know beforehand what topics will be used for the course or which one they'll be assigned.

Resource availability. Adequate resources on a given topic may not be readily available or easily accessible to students. When students pick their own topics, there is no guarantee that sufficient information will be available to complete the assignment. By assigning topics, a professor can help to ensure that adequate resources will be available.

Suggestions

- To help reduce the likelihood of plagiarism, recommend that faculty members alter the lists of topics for their courses every term.
- Suggest that faculty members find a middle ground between assigning topics and allowing students to choose any topic they please by providing a list of topics from which students can pick.
- Ask faculty members to consider replacing a list of suggested research topics with a list of topics that students are not allowed to research. Typically these will be common topics (e.g., death penalty, abortion) that have been written about ad nauseam in the past.

Students Lack Familiarity with Library Resources and Services

Even if students get past the hurdles outlined above, they may still have no idea where to begin seeking information on their topic. In addition to the problems associated with the use of technology as outlined in chapter 4, many students have limited experience working with information and even less experience with academic libraries. As a result, they may not know such basics as when to select a journal article instead of a book or how to determine if a source is peer reviewed.

Suggestions

- Meet with faculty members to discuss search-related problems that have surfaced in the past and develop strategies for eliminating them or reducing their impact on students now or in the future.
- Strongly encourage faculty members to schedule an instruction session with a librarian to familiarize students with the uses, strengths, and weaknesses of common resources (e.g., dictionaries for locating definitions) before students need such information to complete an assignment.
- Consult with faculty members to determine the resources and services students will most likely use to complete a given assignment.

Assignment Requirements Are Unclear or Unspecified

Writing-from-sources and essay assignments typically have very specific requirements. Some of the more common ones include the need for a specified number of sources and restrictions on the nature of sources (e.g., must use peer-reviewed articles, no websites allowed). When such requirements are not specified, it is difficult to know how to provide the best service to students.

Suggestion

- Go over assignments with faculty members before they are distributed to clarify any vague or confusing wordings, requirements, or expectations.

DOS AND DON'TS

As writing-from-sources and essay types of assignments are often precursors to larger, more involved research projects, many of the dos and don'ts that apply to them also apply elsewhere. The following are just a few of the many suggestions that can be shared with faculty as a means of improving written assignments:

DO	DON'T
Be sure students are aware of the different types of essays and which type, if any, is expected to be used for the assignment.	Do not expect students to be familiar with all the types of essays that can be written.
If students are allowed to select their own topics, require topic approval before students actually begin their research to ensure the topics are researchable.	Do not allow students to simply pick any topic that comes to mind.
Give students clear guidelines for picking a researchable topic.	Do not give students the impression that topics are static and don't evolve during the research process.
Provide students with practical suggestions for broadening or narrowing their topics.	Do not allow students to begin research without identifying the perspective they plan to take on their topics.
If topics will be assigned, be sure adequate resources are available for each topic.	Do not assume that the library has adequate resources for every assignment.
When assigning topics, match students with topics that will be personally interesting or relevant (e.g., a topic related to a student's major field of study).	Do not assign topics that reflect your own personal interests or motivations.
Identify resources that are relevant to the content of the course or to the students' chosen fields of study.	Do not assume students will understand the value of a particular library resource or tool once they've accessed it.
Double-check to be sure terms you use are both accurate and current.	Do not assume the terms you've used in the past or that are in use at another library are the same terms currently being used at your library.
Evaluate assignment restrictions and impose only those that have both meaning and purpose.	Do not impose arbitrary assignment restrictions.

SIX TERM/RESEARCH PAPERS

DESCRIPTION

The terms *research paper* and *term paper* are often used interchangeably. However, some people make slight distinctions between the two. For some, a research paper focuses heavily on acquiring information and generating content. Students conduct research on a given topic and present their findings in the form of a paper. Due to their size and the amount of work involved, such projects are usually due later in the term and may also involve some sort of oral or multimedia presentation of the findings.

By contrast, a term paper's focus may or may not be on the actual content. Like a research paper, a term paper involves research and typically takes longer to complete. However, an instructor may use a term paper as a way of gauging things like students' writing progress or their ability to cite sources.

Regardless of which term is used, faculty members may spend time in class discussing the various elements that go into a successful term paper. For example, they may devote time during the first couple of weeks of class to working with students to identify researchable topics and talking about how to access information and evaluate it based on a defined need. Regardless of whether time is spent on preparing students to write a successful paper, the expectations for the final product will vary from faculty member to faculty member. Still, many undergraduate term-paper assignments share some common characteristics, such as

- restrictions on the number of websites that can be cited or otherwise used

- required use of peer-reviewed articles

- specified minimum number of content pages
- specified minimum number of sources to be cited
- submission of a topical outline
- submission of a proposed research strategy
- submission of rough drafts or progress reports throughout the term

TIME FRAME

Given that term papers are typically developed over the course of an academic semester, they are usually due at or near the end of a term. Sometimes a presentation (e.g., PowerPoint) of the project is also required, usually before the paper is submitted. Oftentimes faculty members require parts of a major paper to be submitted throughout the term (e.g., topical outlines, potential search strategies, and rough drafts). This enables them to evaluate student progress, make suggestions, and so on.

INTENDED PURPOSES

Faculty members usually assign term papers for one or two main reasons: to expand students' knowledge about a particular aspect of course content and to familiarize students with the research process.

Content-Oriented Term Papers

Term papers that focus on content may serve as supplements to the material presented in class by motivating students to explore a topic in depth. They may also be used as culminating assignments that enable students to demonstrate their mastery of course content by tying key concepts together into a single project. And, just as often, term papers may be used as independent study projects that lead students to develop knowledge about a course-related topic that was not covered in class.

Research-Focused Term Papers

Some faculty members may use term papers to focus more on the research process than on the written product. For example, rather than expecting students to do a full-blown review of the literature, they may limit students to using only five to ten representative sources. Such an approach shifts the emphasis from the quantity to the quality of the results produced. The students can then focus on conducting better searches and evaluating source material more critically than if they had to find a large number of sources.

WHAT *NOT* TO DO

The examples in this section demonstrate some of the common problems associated with term-paper assignments. Although edited for length, the excerpts are quoted verbatim, and every attempt was made to preserve the flavor and context of the original. The first example is extracted from a content-focused assignment that required students to select a culture other than their own and write a paper about it. In the second sample assignment, content is still an important component, but the main purpose is to have students experience and understand the research process.

Example 1: Content-Focused Term Paper

The assignment below was due in early April and represented 50 percent of a student's final grade for an English 102 course (i.e., typically taken during a student's second semester). The final assignment builds upon three previous research assignments that dealt with (1) notes and note taking, (2) research prospectus, and (3) research terminology/selecting search terms and strategies. The boldface and italics appear in the original.

> Students will write 1 research paper during the semester (*4–5 full, single-spaced pages in length*); the paper must address a topic about a culture other than American culture. At least 5 primary, peer-reviewed academic books and/or academic journals **(print or PDF only)** must be used as sources **(this requirement excludes newspapers, encyclopedias, magazines, HTML text, and websites).**
>
> Research Topics
> Professional conferences have specific themes for research presentation. Since the course will conclude with the research conference, the general theme for class research is **cultural studies.** All research papers must address a specific aspect of a human culture. Below are some suggestions for possible topics.

The syllabus then provides a list of roughly a hundred suggested topics broken down into nine categories.

Problems

Expectations about sources may be overly optimistic. Requiring students to use peer-reviewed source material is admirable, but it creates three potential problems. First, students may not know how to distinguish between an academic, scholarly sort of article and one that's not. Second, they may not have the subject knowledge needed to understand the articles they find. Third, this restriction implies that other sources of information are inferior or inherently inappropriate to the research process. Particularly when students will be using smaller libraries or libraries that have very limited resources, prohibiting them from using sources like encyclopedias and websites may be counterproductive.

Suggested topics are not of interest to students. Suggestions for topics often reflect the instructor's personal or research interests. Students, though, may have little or no interest in those topics. This may add to some students' misperception that research is always about meaningless or irrelevant topics and issues. When students have to research a topic that they're not interested in, the process becomes even more unpleasant for them.

Barring use of HTML text is inappropriate. It is unclear why students are prohibited from using HTML text for the assignment. It may be that the faculty member equates HTML text with websites or assumes that HTML text does not include entire articles. And yet, for all intents and purposes HTML text is the electronic equivalent of the printed article minus the original formatting (e.g., font, columns, pagination).

Revised Example 1

In the revised example, source requirements have been altered. Articles in HTML text are acceptable, as are sources that are not peer reviewed. This is more appropriate to the level and experience of students in an introductory English class.

> Professional conferences have specific themes for research presentations. Because the course will conclude with a mock research conference, the general theme I've selected for class research is "Cultural Studies." Your research paper must address a specific aspect of a human culture that's not your own. Some ideas for possible topics are suggested below.
>
> The term paper will be four to five single-spaced pages in length. *At least* five academic books and/or academic journals must be used as sources. Other sources (e.g., newspapers, encyclopedias, magazines, and websites) may be used to generate topics and ideas. However, such sources are generally not acceptable for professional research conferences. If you wish to use such sources in your final paper, you must speak with me first. Using class discussions about audience, purpose, and other elements of the research process, be prepared to explain why you think one of these sources is more appropriate than a professional, scholarly one.

Example 2: Research-Focused Term Paper

This example also comes from an English 102 course for which a key expectation is that students will complete a term paper. This assignment was distributed in late October. The faculty member appears to be focusing this particular assignment on various elements of the research process (e.g., topic development, interlibrary loan).

Narrow your focus, find information that truly gives you hard data, arguments, reasons, facts, statistics, analyses, counterarguments, opinions (argumentative articles and books)—all useful in the body of your report.

Step I: Guide to Reference Books
Check the *Guide to Reference Books* under your topic area. If you do not find any entries, your topic for this index might be too specific . . . If you come up empty, I want to know why. You should be able to assess this reference source's usefulness for your particular paper topic.

[Step II omitted]

Step III: Interlibrary Loan
Find at least one book or article that is not available from our library but can be ordered via *EZBorrow*. Go through the entire (quick!) process of ordering the book or article. Do this even if the book does not arrive in time to be used in your report.

Problems

Students are required to perform a nonproductive activity. The requirement in step III to find something that is not available is confusing at best and impractical and pedagogically questionable at worst. Resources are not configured to find what a library does not have. A catalog, for example, is designed to show what a library *does* have in its collection. In addition, more and more libraries are incorporating article-linking technology that enables users to see if they can get printed or electronic access to an article when a library doesn't have its original source. In this case, students click on successive links in a result set until they find their desired article. When such technology is not present, students have to complete a number of additional steps to determine an article's availability.

Students may have difficulty applying specific skills to general contexts. Many libraries have a resource (in this example, EZBorrow) that may be used to find and request books (but not articles) from other academic libraries. Available only to schools within a consortium, it enables users to search the catalogs of other member institutions. Users who find a desired book at one of those libraries can submit a request and have the item delivered to their home library. The name of this resource varies from one institution to another. Thus, students who learn to use this resource at one library without fully understanding what it is or when it's to be used may waste time trying to find or use it at another library.

Submitting an actual service request has ripple effects. As noted in the assignment, the process for submitting an interlibrary loan request is quick . . . for the student. However, if course enrollment is large or the faculty member teaches more than one section of the course, more than a hundred students may submit bogus requests. To process all of these requests places an unnecessary burden on library staff and resources. Moreover, if students won't actually use the requested books, they will see the requirement to order an item through interlibrary loan as little more than busywork.

Revised Example 2

In the revised example, students are no longer restricted to using a particular reference book but may choose any that discusses their topic. In addition, they do not have to actually submit an interlibrary loan form. They merely have to complete one and present it to the professor.

> Narrow your focus. Find hard data, arguments, reasons, facts, statistics, analyses, counterarguments, and opinions (argumentative articles and books) that you can use in the body of your report.
>
> **Step I: Finding a reference book on your topic**
> Reference books provide broad overviews of a variety of topics and, as such, are a useful starting point when developing your topic. The library provides access to a number of resources that can be used to identify reference books on your topic. Select your source from the list below. Determine the name of a reference book on (or related to) your proposed topic. Get the book and assess its usefulness for your particular paper. If you can't find any or if the library doesn't have the one you seek, narrow or broaden your search until you find one that's appropriate. Then discuss what you did and why as part of your assessment.
>
> **[Step II omitted]**
>
> **Step III: Interlibrary loan**
> Using a paper form, complete an ILL request for a book or article you think will be useful to you. Do *not* submit the form to the librarian. Bring your completed form to class. Along with your form, submit a summary that tells whether or not our library has the book or article you want and what resource and procedure you used to make this determination.

ISSUES/CONCERNS
Students Lack Familiarity with the Research Process

Many faculty members assume that students have had to complete a term paper in the past or have experience in conducting research. Many students, though, have never been required to complete a term paper. As a result, it is not uncommon to encounter students who have little or no idea where to begin or how to efficiently and successfully progress through the research process. If students do have skills or experience, it is often sketchy. Students may also significantly underestimate the time it takes to conduct research and complete the assignment. Either way, many students have difficulty moving effectively through the necessary steps and, ultimately, bringing everything together into a final, finished product.

Suggestions

- When multiple students seem to be having the same problems with an assignment, attempt to determine who's teaching the course and contact the faculty member about scheduling an instruction session. During instruction, focus on the specific problems encountered by students but also devote some time to discussing the research process and what students can expect next.
- If instruction isn't possible, focus on each student's immediate needs and suggest a one-on-one meeting for follow-up and additional assistance.

Topic Development Is a Common Stumbling Block

One of the key challenges many students face is the lack of a researchable topic. Typically students have a topic that's too broad or too narrow. Many times, they don't realize that they need to identify and consider factors that might influence their research (e.g., perspective, time period, gender). As a result, they struggle with what search terms and resources to use to find the information they seek. Conversely, in cases where faculty members assign topics, the library may lack the resources to meet the students' needs.

Suggestions

- Encourage faculty members to require students to submit detailed topic proposals before conducting their initial searches.
- Before students begin their research, suggest that they develop a list of alternative spellings, related concepts, and so on relevant to their topic.
- Work with faculty members who assign topics to ensure that adequate library resources are available for students to complete their papers as expected.

A Required Resource Is Dated or Unavailable

Many professors use research primers and other textbooks to introduce students to the library and to the research process. These resources often indicate "standard" sources that can be found in "every library." However, no library can have every possible source. Other possibilities are that the library's edition may be different from the one cited, it may be dated or otherwise inappropriate, or it may even be signed out.

Suggestions

- Be sure the required resources are available before an assignment is distributed.
- Determine if alternative resources are acceptable. For example, many times a similar work or an earlier edition is acceptable, but students don't think to use it or aren't aware of it.

DOS AND DON'TS

The following are just a few of the many suggestions that can be shared with faculty as a means of improving the assignment of term or research papers:

DO	DON'T
Gear content expectations to the level of the students in the class.	Do not restrict students to a particular format of text—printed, HTML, or PDF.
Be clear about source limitations (e.g., date range, scholarly or nonscholarly).	Do not expect students to be able to tell the difference between a scholarly resource and a nonscholarly one.
Determine whether or not alternative editions or similar sources are acceptable.	Do not assume that required resources are available in the library.
Suggest students pick topics that are of interest or relevant to their chosen discipline or career path.	Do not assign students (particularly first-year students) topics for which the library has few, if any, resources.
Before students start to look for source material, work with them to develop a researchable topic.	Do not have students start the research process until they have a clear idea of their topic.
Make students aware of library resources and services (e.g., interlibrary loan) that can assist them in accessing hard-to-find source material.	Do not require students to use a particular service unless and until it's appropriate.

SEVEN CITING SOURCES AND INFORMATION ETHICS

DESCRIPTION

Citing sources isn't so much an assignment as a part of an assignment, but a discussion of it is included because source citations are called for in so many types and levels of assignments. Citing sources has two components. The first is knowing how to record source information through note taking, quoting, and paraphrasing. The second is knowing how to present various pieces of bibliographic information in a prescribed sequence and format in order to give proper credit for material that is not one's own. Typically source citations will appear in the form of footnotes, a bibliography, or a works cited page. Because citations are related to the source material that emerges during the research process, their use is typically associated with assignments involving research. Both writing-from-sources and essay assignments (see chapters 5 and 6) may require some sort of citation for the sources used.

TIME FRAME

Depending on an instructor's expectations, students may find that formatting citations can be one of the most painstaking and time-consuming parts of an assignment. Because the list of references or page of works cited typically appears at the end of a paper, it is often submitted at or near the end of the term or as part of the final assignment.

INTENDED PURPOSES

There are several reasons why faculty members require students to cite the sources they have used. Three of the most common are

1. To prompt discussion of some of the ethical and legal issues surrounding the use of information

2. To demonstrate how the elements of a proper citation help in accessing and retrieving required information

3. To familiarize students with scholarly publications and academic writing

THE CHALLENGES
Students Lack Experience in Using Citations

It cannot be assumed that students know how to format and cite information sources. Many students arrive at college with little or no experience writing research papers or providing properly formatted citations. In fact, many upper-level undergraduate students may be equally unfamiliar with how to properly cite sources of information. Many students simply don't understand the need to give credit for work that isn't their own. And students who do understand the need may well be baffled by how to cite sources from the ever-changing world of electronic and web-based information.

Suggestions
- Faculty members must be made aware of the varied levels of experience students bring to class with respect to properly using and citing source material.
- Identify common elements in citations and stress consistency within whichever style is used, especially if a student is unfamiliar with how to style citations in the first place.

Students Don't Know How to Cite Information Properly

Along similar lines, students are often unfamiliar with the various ways of properly incorporating source material into their work. The copying and pasting of text, pictures, and so on into a paper has become a common practice. And yet, many students are completely unaware of or are indifferent to the need to cite sources when using material that's not their own. In addition, students who are aware of the need may not know how citations should be employed.

Arranged from most specific to general, table 7.1 provides a broad overview of the three ways in which source material is typically incorporated into a document. There are numerous sources that provide additional details about each technique and how to instruct students in their proper use.

Suggestion

■ Provide students with examples of how and when to paraphrase, quote, or summarize other people's work.

Students Have Difficulty Transferring from One Citation Style to Another

Even if students have learned what to cite and when, they may not be familiar with the citation style being used in a given course. For example, while in high school they may have used the Turabian or Chicago style for all of their work. But they may now be required to use both Modern Language Association style (e.g., in English 101) and American Psychological Association style (e.g., in Psychology 101) in a single semester. This can be extremely confusing and frustrating.

Suggestion

■ When working with faculty members who have no strongly preferred citation style, suggest that they encourage students to use the style associated with their major/discipline whenever possible.

TABLE 7.1 **PRIMARY TECHNIQUES FOR INCORPORATING SOURCE MATERIAL**

The example for each technique is based on the statement, "Skin cancer is generally divided into two main classes, nonmelanomas and melanomas, both types affecting different types of skin cells" (Joyce 2007, 143).

TECHNIQUE	DESCRIPTION	EXAMPLE
Quoting	Exact words used in the original are placed in quotation marks.	"Skin cancer is generally divided into two main classes."
Paraphrasing	Information from a source is restated in a way that retains the essence of the original statement without quoting it word for word.	There are two primary types of skin cancer.
Summarizing	Key points from the source material are rewritten in a more succinct, more focused way in the student's own words.	The type of skin cell affected depends on the type of skin cancer.

Faculty Members Often Have Unclear or Mixed Expectations

One of the biggest problems with assignments involving the citation of source material is that the instructor's expectations about citations are unclear. Citation requirements can be confusing in a number of ways.

Ambiguous grading criteria. Although complete and proper citations are often listed as an element that will affect a paper's grade, many times it is not clear to what extent or how such material is to be graded. For example, will a percentage be subtracted for every citation that contains one or more errors or for every error that is made? Similarly, it is often unclear how stringent the instructor will be. Will a percentage be deducted, for example, each time a particular type of error is made or only the first time?

Instructor's lack of knowledge. Sometimes faculty members don't keep up with changes in citation format. In such cases, the faculty member either doesn't check or isn't aware of inaccuracies in the students' citations. This is especially true for citations of electronic and web-based information.

Indifference to citing sources and making citations. Faculty indifference to citing sources and citation styles may manifest itself in any of a number of ways. For example, it is not uncommon for instructors to require research without requiring citations or at least a list of references. An even bigger problem arises when faculty members don't check to see if the sources used by students actually exist and the details are accurate. As a result, they cannot properly assess whether the citations are complete or correct.

Suggestion

- Speak with faculty members one-on-one to determine their specific expectations with regard to the citing of source material.

Students Lack Awareness of the Consequences of Improperly Cited Source Material

Most, if not all, colleges and universities have some sort of policy regarding plagiarism and the submission of work that's not a student's own. Those policies can typically be found in a variety of publications, such as the institution's undergraduate catalog and the student handbook. Failing the course in which the plagiarized work was submitted or even expulsion are among the more severe penalties that are typically imposed. Unfortunately, some instructors are unfamiliar with or choose to ignore such sanctions and never take action when students submit plagiarized work.

Suggestion

- At the very least, faculty members need to inform students of their policies and the consequences of submitting plagiarized material. An instructor's approach should be consistent with the institution's policies and penalties.

The Use of Term-Paper Factories Is on the Rise

One of the more troublesome and problematic developments in academia is student use of term-paper factories. Although the level and variety of services vary, the key service that the majority of these websites provides is access to previously written works. This can range anywhere from admission application letters to term papers and even to dissertations. Some sites even guarantee they will write a paper for the student that's "plagiarism free."

Suggestions

- Develop students' awareness of campus policies and possible consequences regarding plagiarism and the submission of work that's not one's own.
- Learn about plagiarism-detecting software and websites (e.g., Turnitin.com) and publicize their existence to students and faculty.

Students Use Technology to Embed Citations and Create Bibliographies

Many electronic information resources allow citation information to be downloaded directly. Productivity software applications (e.g., Word) are becoming increasingly sophisticated with respect to importing and producing properly formatted citation information. But, despite these advances, no software is 100 percent reliable. Citations should still be checked for accuracy. Some of the common problems associated with the use of these technologies include the following:

- The original citation information is incorrect, incomplete, or not formatted in a way that is compatible with the citation software being used.

- The student is unfamiliar with how to use the software effectively.

- Older software may not have all of the current formatting algorithms needed to produce accurate citations.

- Many applications do not check for spelling or typographical errors that can occur when users enter citation information themselves.

Suggestion

- Hold workshops where students and faculty can learn about available citation software and technologies and the specific strengths and weaknesses associated with using them.

CITATION STYLES

There are dozens of citation styles and conventions. Even though each discipline focuses on different elements, most citation styles have many elements in common (e.g., author's name, publication year). And yet, each style is distinctly different in both the order and the manner in which information is presented. Adding to the complexity is the fact that many journals have their own specific expectations about citing source material. Thus, it is not surprising that students often become confused about what to cite and how. This confusion and frustration can increase exponentially if a student is taking two or more courses that require different citation styles.

Suggestions

- Work with faculty members to determine what constitutes a proper citation for any given assignment. Although some instructors expect 100 percent accuracy, most allow some flexibility and focus more on consistency and content than on the format of citations.
- Develop a list of style guides and citation resources available in the library and online.

Examples of Citation Styles

Three of the most commonly used style guides/publication manuals are published by the American Psychological Association, the University of Chicago Press, and the Modern Language Association:

American Psychological Association. 2009. *Publication Manual of the American Psychological Association.* 6th ed. Washington, DC: American Psychological Association.

The Chicago Manual of Style. 15th ed. 2003. Chicago: University of Chicago Press.

Modern Language Association. 2009. *MLA Handbook for Writers of Research Papers.* 7th ed. New York: Modern Language Association.

Table 7.2 compares the ways APA, Chicago, and MLA sequence citation information for three basic types of publications. To view sequencing for additional kinds of publications as well as exact formatting conventions and specifications (e.g., indentation), please refer to the appropriate style manual.

TABLE 7.2   SAMPLE SOURCE CITATIONS IN THREE STYLES

LOCATION IN MANUAL		SAMPLE CITATION
Journal Article		
APA	Journal article without DOI (3b, p. 199)	Light, M. A., & Light, I. H. (2008). The geographic expansion of Mexican immigration in the United States and its implications for local law enforcement. *Law Enforcement Executive Forum Journal, 8*(1), 73–82.
	Journal article with DOI (1, p. 198)	Herbst-Damm, K. L., & Kulik, J. A. (2005). Volunteer support, marital status, and the survival times of terminally ill patients. *Health Psychology, 24,* 225–229. doi: 10.1037/0278-6133.24.2.225
Chicago	Journal article (17.151, p. 688)	Calabrese, E. J., and L. A. Baldwin. 1999. Reevaluation of the fundamental close-response relationship. *BioScience* 49:725–32.
MLA	Article in scholarly journal (5.4.2, p. 137)	Piper, Andrew. "Rethinking the Print Object: Goethe and the Book of Everything." *PMLA* 121.1 (2006): 124–38. Print.
Book		
APA	Entire book, print version (18, p. 203)	Shotton, M. A. (1989). *Computer addiction? A study of computer dependency.* London, England: Taylor & Francis.
Chicago	Book, one author (17.26, p. 649)	Martin du Gard, Roger. *Lieutenant-Colonel de Maumort.* Translated by Luc Brébion and Timothy Crouse. New York: Alfred A. Knopf, 2000.
MLA	Book by a single author (5.5.2, p. 149)	Franke, Damon. *Modernist Heresies: British Literary History, 1883–1924.* Columbus: Ohio State UP, 2008. Print.
Web Sources		
APA	Blog post (76a, p. 215)	PZ Myers. (2007, January 22). The unfortunate prerequisites and consequences of partitioning your mind [Web log post]. Retrieved from http://scienceblogs.com/pharyngula/2007/01/the _unfortunate_prerequisites.php.

(cont.)

TABLE 7.2 (cont.)

LOCATION IN MANUAL		SAMPLE CITATION
Chicago	Website, owner of site used for author (17.237, p. 715)	Federation of American Scientists. Resolution comparison: Reading license plates and headlines. http://www.fas.org/irp/imint/resolve5.htm.
MLA	Web publication (5.6.1, p. 182)	Eaves, Morris, Robert Essick, and Joseph Viscomi, eds. *The William Blake Archive.* Lib. of Cong., 28 Sept. 2007. Web. 20 Nov. 2007. <http://www.blakearchive.org/blake/>.

EIGHT ASSIGNMENTS IN THE ONLINE ENVIRONMENT

DESCRIPTION

Many of the challenges that students encounter with assignments involving the library are no different from those they face in the online environment. Whether students are enrolled in an online course or working on a project from home, problems with incorrect terminology, inaccurate citations, and other issues discussed throughout this book are likely to arise. Similarly, whether working online or in the library, students often struggle with deciding where to begin, which resource to use, how to use it, and so on. That said, the online environment does pose some unique challenges to faculty members attempting to incorporate online research into their assignments as well as to students trying to complete those assignments.

THE NEED

As the ability to provide remote access to library resources and services has grown, so too have user expectations for greater and increasingly seamless access. Part of this certainly reflects an evolution in the way both society and individuals perceive and deal with information and education. But an equal if not greater role can be attributed to the rapid growth in the number and variety of courses being developed for and administered online. In fact, the overwhelming majority of four-year colleges and universities offer some form of online or distributed learning courses. Many of the students enrolled in these courses rarely come to campus, if they come to campus at all. Nonetheless, they expect that the resources they need to complete such courses will be readily available. As a result, whether students are in an online course or just accessing resources remotely, faculty members need to be aware of the challenges involved in the remote use of library resources and services to work on assignments. They can then create more effective assignments as well as provide a higher level of assistance when their students request help.

TECHNICAL CHALLENGES

Many of the technical difficulties students experience with traditional assignments (see chapter 12) also occur with assignments online. Some of those challenges take on their own unique twist in the online environment.

Students Don't Know How to Access Resources and Course Materials Off-Site

As more and more institutions adopt a single, universal sign-on procedure, remote access is becoming increasingly seamless and transparent for many resources and services. However, there are still many institutions where these technologies are not yet in place or fully implemented across campus. As a result, students might need to know how to use several accounts with different user names, passwords, and procedures to access library resources and services effectively and efficiently.

Suggestions

- Provide faculty members with a list of remotely accessible resources and services, log-in procedures, and access points/URLs. Be especially clear about the procedures for the resources students need for a particular course or assignment.
- Be sure that students are being referred to online resources that are available via the host institution. Articles in databases to which the library doesn't subscribe, for example, cannot be accessed by students or faculty.

Pop-Up, Firewall, and Other Security Applications May Affect Resource Functionality

Fortunately, security applications that interfere with a resource's functionality are becoming increasingly rare. And yet, when remote users report problems, they are sometimes the result of a security setting that is too high. For example, result lists from a database search may not appear if pop-ups are blocked and the result page is considered a pop-up.

Suggestion

- Because library databases are essentially secure sites, there is no need to have more than basic security (e.g., low to medium) settings in place. However, users need to be aware that if they go beyond a resource (i.e., onto the Web), they will need to adjust their security settings.

Inadequate or Inappropriate Computer Configurations May Create Problems

Sometimes it's a student's computer that is causing access and usage problems. Unfortunately, everyone's computer is configured differently. As a result, it is impossible to anticipate every possible problem students might need to address. Exacerbating the situation are the facts that computers are continually being updated and that people frequently install new software and hardware, both of which create subtle changes to systems. In many cases, the user is unaware that changes have been made, what the changes were, and how they may affect usage. Sometimes getting one application or tool to work requires sacrificing functionality in another application or tool, particularly with hardware and software designed for use on older machines and systems.

Suggestion
- Where applicable, inform faculty members of recommended settings, preferred software configurations, and similar technical information that facilitates online access.

Students with Dial-Up Access May Be Unable to Use Certain Library Resources and Services

In the age of wireless technology, the limitations of dial-up access may seem like an outdated issue. However, in many rural areas, dial-up service may be the only way to access the Internet. The slowness of dial-up access can severely affect student performance. Some library services may be limited or unavailable to dial-up users, and large files may take a long time to download, if they can be downloaded at all.

Suggestion
- Remind faculty members that some students still use dial-up services to connect to the Internet, which may make it difficult or even impossible for them to download large files, view videos properly, and so on.

Some Resources and Services May Not Be Available Off-Site

Resources and services may be unavailable off-site for a number of reasons. Sometimes resources go down without warning. Fortunately, these instances are few and far between. A system or resource is more likely to be down because of a planned outage, service upgrade, or software update. Some libraries hosting resources locally may take them off-line for similar reasons. Such lapses may affect distance students more than students on campus, who can still attend classes and use the library.

Although it is becoming more the exception than the rule, some online resources may be available only in the library or on campus via a networked computer. As discussed in chapter 3, some of those resources may require librarian mediation (e.g., log-in) for access. In addition, some licensing arrangements permit only a specified number of concurrent users. For example, if access is limited to fifty users, when that number is reached, an additional student will not be able to access the software until a current user exits.

Suggestions

- Give advance notification of planned outages to faculty teaching online courses so that they can prepare students for what they are likely to encounter when trying to complete an assignment.
- Be sure that faculty members are aware of library-only resources and that appropriate information is incorporated into any literature or website about resource access.
- Have faculty remind students to log out of resources when they're finished using them.
- Explore ways of making books and other library items available to students.

Software Incompatibility Can Cause Problems for Instructors and Students Alike

Some would argue that software incompatibility is not necessarily a library-related issue. However, that argument is increasingly dubious on at least two levels. First, the format of many files used to store information (e.g., PDF, Flash) often requires special software for access and use. Second, many items that faculty used to place on reserve in the library are now being placed on electronic reserve. Depending on the format of these items, students may not be able to access or otherwise work on them. Students, for example, may complete and submit their assignments in a format that's not readable on a faculty member's computer or may complete an assignment only to find they can't present it on the computer in the lab or classroom. They may experience similar problems opening and working on their files in the library. Information downloaded into a presentation, for example, may require a newer version of Shockwave or other software in order to open and be viewed properly. As much as possible, libraries should strive to maintain the current versions of all software and install all possible upgrades and patches so that information retrieved in the library can be manipulated in the library.

Suggestions

- Suggest faculty create and save files in the lowest common denominator format—the format requiring the least amount of effort to access and use.
- Work with faculty members to develop a list of preferred software to be used by students and to be installed in the classroom or lab where students will be expected to present their completed assignments, give presentations, and so on. This list should be included in the syllabus and in pertinent assignments.
- Create a web page of links to viewers, plug-ins, and other software and downloads that might be needed by students to complete their assignments.

ONLINE-SPECIFIC CHALLENGES

When working with online learners—whether students taking courses online or students using library resources and services remotely—there are a number of things librarians need to consider. Although some of these considerations apply to on-campus situations, they are particularly relevant when dealing with students completing assignments from an off-site location.

Deciding Which Technologies to Use to Communicate with Students

As information technologies continue to evolve, librarians are faced with the growing challenge of deciding how best to communicate with online learners as they work on their assignments. Because many of these students may not be able to come to the library for face-to-face assistance, a decision has to be made about which technologies will be most effective. E-mail, telephone, and web pages are still commonly used in most libraries. However, some libraries now employ proprietary reference management software (e.g., QuestionPoint), and many more have begun to incorporate new and emergent technologies such as blogs, instant messaging, wikis, and Facebook to interact with online students.

Once a decision has been made about technologies, administration becomes a key challenge to address. For example, the screen size, resolution, and memory of many devices (e.g., cell phones) may render it impossible to run certain applications or properly view things such as web pages. A related problem is that as more technologies are used, more time and resources are required to update and maintain them. For this reason, many libraries are forced to find some sort of balance between trying to be all things to all users and doing a few simple things well.

Suggestions

- Provide a menu of static (e.g., web pages) and dynamic (e.g., instant messaging) technology options to accommodate as many learners and learning styles as is practical.
- Start with technologies that are inexpensive and easy to use and expand as resources and demand allow.
- Alert faculty members to the types and locations of assistance provided to online learners by the library and librarians.

Deciding How to Provide Instruction

No matter what technologies are in place, online learners need to know where to find them and, more important, how to use them. Instruction thus becomes a critical issue. Many of the questions that arise will be very similar. Like on-campus students, online learners often don't know which resources to use or how to properly construct a search strategy. And yet, despite the similarities, students will all have their own unique needs. Some will have very specific questions that can be answered quickly, and others will need a more lengthy and detailed set of instructions.

Suggestions

- Develop training and awareness-raising activities for faculty in the use of databases and electronic communication software (e.g., instant messaging) used by librarians to assist online learners.
- Work with faculty members to decide the best ways of providing instruction to online students.

Deciding What Amount of Support to Provide

In the online environment, it might take significantly greater amounts of both time and patience to address students' needs. A student, for example, may send an instant message (IM) saying nothing more than "I'm having problems finding information on my topic." It may take several IMs before the librarian understands what specific information is needed. It may then take several more IMs to actually teach the student how to conduct a search, navigate result lists, and so on. Because of the ease of access, some online learners may even expect the librarian to send them articles and web links to material, thereby adding another layer of complexity to the exchange. Even if the librarian is a fast typist, a single transaction could still take several minutes or even hours before it has been completed successfully.

Suggestions

- Decide the best ways to address specific, commonly asked questions versus those involving more lengthy, detailed instruction.
- Articulate the roles of both faculty members and librarians in providing support.
- Be clear that librarians are not available to do the students' work for them.

Deciding How to Alert Librarians That a Student Is Part of a Class

In general, librarians should do their best to help anyone requesting assistance and shouldn't make a distinction between traditional learners using online resources and learners enrolled in online courses. In some libraries, though, a librarian is embedded, or assigned to work with students in specific courses. Arguably, those librarians' first responsibility is to provide assistance to students enrolled in the courses to which they're assigned. In such cases, when an IM or e-mail comes to a librarian's desk, it needs to be clear whether the student is enrolled in an assigned course or just someone working online.

Suggestions

- Alert faculty members to which librarians—if any—are assigned to assist online students.
- Suggest students identify the course in question and the instructor in the subject line of a message or in the initial correspondence (e.g., "? for EDUC788, Dr. Smith").
- Be sure online students know the preferred methods (e.g., e-mail, instant message) and times for contacting the librarian assigned to work with their class.

Monitoring Students to See If They're Doing Their Own Work

Checking that online students' work has been ethically produced is a two-step process. The first step is determining whether or not students are actually the ones doing the work they've been assigned. That task is problematic enough in traditional courses. The fact that instructors rarely, if ever, see students in online courses complicates the matter, and the advent of online term-paper mills adds to the complexity. Simply put, there is no definitive way to determine whether students themselves did the work assigned. That responsibility falls outside the realm of a librarian's duties and abilities.

However, librarians can play a role in the second step of the process: detecting plagiarism. It is not uncommon for faculty members to contact librarians about checking students' citations. The task may be as simple as verifying the accuracy of a particular citation. Or it may involve comparing the text a student has submitted against the original source to see if plagiarism has occurred and to what degree. The use of plagiarism-detecting software and websites (e.g., Turnitin.com) is becoming increasingly common on many campuses. See chapter 7 for additional information on plagiarism and citing sources.

PART IV BRIDGE COLLAPSE!
Library Assignments That Fail

NINE TOURS

DESCRIPTION

Tours are used as a means of educating students about the location of and access points to library resources, services, and personnel. Just about anything—from the location of the reference desk to the software available on various computers—can be the focus of a tour. A traditional tour is designed to show groups a broad cross section of what the library has to offer. A custom tour is geared to a group's specific needs, wants, and interests. Although librarians are often asked to give tours as part of a course, admissions and other offices and groups on campus may also give tours of the library—with or without the library's input.

Tours are typically offered in one of four formats: guided, self-paced, textual, and virtual. Each has its own advantages and disadvantages, as outlined in table 9.1.

TIME FRAME

The time needed to complete a tour varies. Among other things, it will depend on the type of tour, what's covered, and the size of the tour group. That said, no type of tour should take longer to complete than any other. For example, if a virtual tour of your library takes thirty minutes, a guided tour should not take any longer. Looked at in another way, why would anyone undertake a guided tour if it takes twice as long to complete as a virtual one?

TABLE 9.1   ADVANTAGES AND DISADVANTAGES OF FOUR TYPES OF TOURS

TYPE OF TOUR	DESCRIPTION	ADVANTAGES	DISADVANTAGES
Guided	Librarian or staff member serves as guide and moderator, walking with the group through the library	• Questions can be addressed directly and immediately • Guide controls tour's pace and content	• Takes time to coordinate and administer • Can be noisy and disruptive • Presents logistical challenges (e.g., time for large group to move from one floor to another)
Self-paced	Student proceeds at own pace through prescribed areas and tour points	• Individual can proceed at own pace • Requires minimal staff time and resources	• User may not spend enough time on key elements or may miss or even skip them
Textual	Student follows a written guide identifying key resources and services; a variation of self-paced tours	• Every student receives the same information.	• Needs to be updated on a regular basis • One size fits all may not meet all students' needs
Virtual	Student uses software to view prescribed areas; sometimes student can experience specific features, resources, or services	• Provides same information every time • Individual can generally proceed at own pace • Requires minimal staff involvement and resources	• Maintenance requires knowledge of software and person to make changes • Advanced software features may go unused to keep tour user-friendly • Often lacks capacity to provide quick answers to questions

INTENDED PURPOSES

At the most basic level, the purpose of a tour is to expose participants to the physical location of library resources and services. Tours also have the advantage of making it possible to convey information in a systematic, consistent manner to large groups of people. Thus, it is not uncommon for tours to be part of recruitment efforts, alumni gatherings, and similar institutional activities. Tours may also play a role in class assignments. It is not uncommon for faculty members, for example, to require first-year students to complete a library tour as a way of getting them into the library and giving them an overview of the resources and services the library has to offer.

Many libraries are taking advantage of the Internet and other technologies to create virtual tours that accomplish the same goals as other kinds of tours. The use of technology offers opportunities for incorporating elements that would be difficult or even impossible to include in a face-to-face tour. For example, in a virtual tour students could not only be shown where to locate the catalog but also be asked to actually access it and search for a book. Students on a face-to-face tour could be asked to do the same, but a limited number of computers, time considerations, and other factors would make such interactive, hands-on activities problematic at best.

WHAT *NOT* TO DO

Because every library is different, it would be difficult to provide a meaningful critique of a script for a face-to-face or virtual tour. For this reason, an actual written, sixteen-page guide was selected and used as the basis of the discussion contained in this section. The guide in question was distributed in January 2003 and in 2008. Based on the title on its cover—*Library Research in Criminal Justice*—it was apparently distributed to criminal justice students. However, it remains unclear if it was distributed to incoming freshmen, to students in a particular course, or to every student majoring in criminal justice. It is equally unclear when this guide was first distributed, how often it has been distributed, and if it is still being distributed.

In any case, this guide's greatest flaw is the dated information it contains. At best, much of the information is misleading. At worst, the information is incorrect. The following represent some of the more serious defects in the 2008 version:

- Much of the text was copied from the library's web pages and, as a result, some of the text (e.g., "Click here") wasn't intended to appear in printed form and makes reading the hard copy awkward.

- Nearly two entire pages are devoted to six "Traditional Hard Copy Indexes." The library's subscriptions to all but one were canceled prior to 1994. Even if students were expected to use the available editions, the guide fails to identify their location in the library.

- The version of the library's home page portrayed in the guide has since been revised twice, and many of the screen shots used as examples are equally dated.

- The URL to the library's list of databases is incorrect. Moreover, the text states that the library has dozens when in fact the library provides access to more than a hundred databases. Worst of all? The only place the database Criminal Justice Abstracts is mentioned at all in this self-described guide to library research in criminal justice is on this list of 75+ resources and, even then, only its name is provided. Readers are given no information about content, coverage, tips for searching, and so on.

Problems

The rationale for focusing on printed indexes is unclear. That a guide to resources related to criminal justice talks about printed indexes without even mentioning the availability of the electronic version of Criminal Justice Abstracts as a search tool is a grave oversight. This is not to say that printed indexes are not valuable resources. However, the value of including them seems dubious, especially given the age of such resources and the wide array of other resources to which students have access. Starting the research guide with a discussion of printed indexes seems equally inappropriate and risks attributing undue importance or usefulness for them.

Inaccuracies and misinformation compromise credibility. In using this guide, students would quickly learn of its shortcomings. At the very least, confusing and often incorrect information raises the question of whether the authors know what they're talking about. If students perceive librarians were involved in the creation of the guide, it could cast the library in a negative light as well.

Bad information requires a reeducating of students. When students are given the wrong information, a librarian must reeducate them when they come to the library and ask for assistance. Unfortunately, not every student seeks help. Especially in those that don't, the misinformation could create persistent bad habits and cause untold confusion and frustration down the road. Additionally, the situation puts a librarian in the awkward position of having to correct or otherwise contradict information the students were given by their professor. Although some professors are appreciative of feedback, many see any criticism as presumptuous and intrusive. This can be particularly true at institutions where librarians do not hold faculty status.

ISSUES/CONCERNS
Quality Suffers When Tours Aren't Given by a Librarian

Even faculty members who are frequent users of the library are prone to misspeaking about or misrepresenting library resources and services. This is usually completely innocent and tends to result from unawareness of changes that have occurred or limited familiarity with a resource or service. Some, though, may point out only what they feel is important or useful, regardless of student or assignment needs. This can give students a very myopic, lopsided view of the library and its usefulness.

Suggestions

- Provide faculty members with a list of new things prior to the start of every term to assist them in updating their tour presentations.
- Meet with faculty members who conduct tours to review scripts on a regular basis.
- Prepare and distribute a tour script to help ensure that key resources and services are discussed and that accurate information is shared.

Tours Generally Don't Discuss the Hows, Only the Wheres

Dated and inaccurate information aside, perhaps the biggest problem with tours is that their focus is misplaced. They show students where to go for things like reference assistance or to sign out a book but offer little (if any) opportunity for discussing how to use a particular resource or service. The increasing number and availability of electronic resources and services only exacerbate this problem. Even so, many librarians and faculty members would agree that learning how to use a resource or service is outside the scope of a traditional tour.

Suggestion

- Suggest to faculty that perhaps a tour is not the best use of students' time. Instead, recommend an instruction session during which key resources *and* how to use them will be the focus.

Choosing What Information to Present Can Be Difficult

Deciding which topics to emphasize and which to sacrifice is a difficult balancing act. Whether a tour is general or designed to meet a specific course need, some topics must necessarily be overlooked or, at best, only discussed in a cursory manner. Even though there simply isn't enough time to cover every possible resource and service, the inclusion/exclusion of something or the amount of attention paid to a particular area can be interpreted to mean that some things are more important than others.

Suggestions

- Begin by focusing a tour on the needs of a specific assignment. As time permits, include other information.
- Be sure to indicate that the tour is an overview only, that it does not and cannot possibly include discussion about every resource and service your library has to offer.

Getting a Group through the Library Poses Numerous Logistical Problems

Even a small group of just five to ten people can create a number of obstacles to a successful tour. Simply getting the entire group up the stairs or elevator, for example, can be a time-consuming process. Plans must be in place to ensure that individuals in wheelchairs or with other disabilities will be able to participate in the tour and any related activities. Other tour-related issues that need to be considered include how to deal with increased noise, disruptive/distracting behavior, poor acoustics, and time constraints.

Suggestion

- Decide which parts of the tour can be pointed to or discussed without actually going to that area or floor. For example, you could show students where the computer lab is without actually having them all walk in and out.

Tours Reinforce the Idea of Library as Place

Tours reinforce the idea that the library is a place rather than a point of access. Granted, libraries do provide access to a wealth of information, resources, and services not available elsewhere. However, given the ever-growing array of electronic resources and access methods available, focusing on the physical aspects of the library is increasingly anachronistic and, in many ways, a disservice to students.

Suggestions

- Make it a point to highlight off-site accessibility and alternative formats (e.g., printed and electronic versions of journals).
- Create an off-site or distance education page highlighting what resources and services are available outside the library and how to gain access.

Tours Often Lack Relevance and Usefulness to Students

In the end, librarians and faculty members really need to examine the educational value of a tour. Although tours are not without merit, in many ways the shortcomings may outweigh the benefits. Tours are often seen as inherently valuable in and of themselves. As a result, faculty may require students to take tours even when their courses have no library-related assignments. As with any assignment, a tour without a context is quickly perceived as little more than busywork by students, and its value is diminished exponentially.

Because they have long played a role in library instruction, tours hold a lot of sentimental value for many librarians. Combined with the high visibility that tours generate for the library, many librarians are loathe to stop providing them as a service to the campus community. But, to paraphrase the words of a colleague at another library that no longer gives tours, "We're a library, not a museum. If students need to know where to sign out books or where the photocopiers are located, they'll ask. We need to focus our time and resources on teaching students *how* to use the library, not *where* things are in the library."

Suggestions

- Suggest alternatives to tours, particularly when tours are proposed as academic assignments.
- If it is decided that a tour is indeed the best approach, librarians should work closely with instructors to identify ways of creating tours that are relevant to a particular course, assignment, or group of students.

SOME COMMENTS ON VIRTUAL TOURS

As noted earlier, virtual tours have some advantages over their face-to-face counterparts. They also overcome some of the challenges of face-to-face tours (e.g., lack of consistency). However, virtual tours have their own unique shortcomings as well.

Questionable transferability. It is unclear if information presented in a virtual tour truly transfers to the physical library. For example, when students who have taken a virtual tour visit the library for the first time, they may find that the actual circulation desk looks nothing like the one depicted in the virtual tour.

Lack of personal contact. During a virtual tour, there is often no one directly available to answer questions or with whom to otherwise interact. Many virtual tours incorporate chat or other forms of instant messaging, but those technologies can be cumbersome and tedious for complex or lengthy questions. Moreover, a librarian giving a face-to-face tour can often add personal insights or details that add relevance and levity.

Linear nature of virtual tours. Many virtual tours are linear. That is, they start and stop at a certain point and progress in a straight line from point A to point B. Depending on the sophistication of the software and the person who created the tour, students may not have the opportunity to skip already-known information. Or they may not be able to stop and start the tour at will. If they don't finish it in one sitting, for example, they may have to go through the entire tour again.

Faulty or insufficient technology. Obviously, a virtual tour is dependent upon the technology on which it is built as well as on the technology with which it is accessed. If the server goes down, for example, no one will be able to access the virtual tour until the server is operational again. Likewise, depending on how a tour is constructed, students working from home computers may not be able to use it in the way it was intended. Graphics and animations, for example, may not function properly.

DOS AND DON'TS

The value of a tour as an academic assignment is questionable at best. As noted earlier, although a tour may show students where to find things in the library, it does not provide the skills library users need to navigate the variety of information resources available to them. When tours are given, it is strongly suggested that they be related to some larger project or subsequent assignment. The lack of a context in which students can use what they learn quickly diminishes the value of a tour and ultimately defeats the purpose of providing a tour in the first place.

The following are just a few of the many suggestions that can be shared with faculty as ways of improving tours of the library:

DO	DON'T
Regularly provide updated information to all potential tour guides.	Do NOT assume that information presented on previous tours is still accurate and up-to-date.
Standardize content so that all tour guides speak about the same things.	Do NOT allow tour guides to pick and choose what they'd like to talk about on a tour.
Develop a list of commonly asked questions (and answers) that can be shared with tour guides.	Do NOT assume tour guides will know how to answer every question they might be asked.
Supply a script to all potential tour guides.	Do NOT encourage tour guides to wing it. Although this adds a personal touch, the information shared is often biased, misleading, and, in some cases, inaccurate.
Focus tour stops on assignments or elements most relevant to students' course or discipline.	
When nonlibrarians give tours, try to be involved in the planning and administration process to ensure good information.	Do NOT offer to give a tour without some sort of context or assignment to which it can be directed.
Review virtual tours on a regular basis to ensure the currency and accuracy of their content.	Do NOT let incorrect or misleading information go unheeded. Contact the appropriate person or department to offer helpful suggestions for improving their tours.
	Do NOT assume that a virtual tour will work on every machine students use.

TEN SCAVENGER HUNTS

DESCRIPTION

Library scavenger hunts (or seek-and-finds as they are sometimes called) are based on a faculty-provided list of things that students are to locate, discover, use, or identify. The list may consist of specific items (e.g., books), resources, services, personnel, and other information at the library. In this sense, scavenger hunts are very much like tours, except that students are expected to complete them on their own and at their own pace. At their simplest, scavenger hunts are general and straightforward. However, they can be customized for a particular class or assignment. Many faculty members see these types of assignments as nonthreatening, fun ways to introduce students to the library. For this reason, they are often used in introductory courses or freshman-year experience activities in which it is presumed students have little or no understanding of the library.

TIME FRAME

As with all assignments, the time frame for completing a scavenger hunt varies from one course to another. Faculty often perceive that relatively little time is needed to complete a scavenger hunt, and some expect the results to be completed and turned in as early as the next class. A more reasonable expectation is one to two weeks.

INTENDED PURPOSES

Scavenger hunts may be designed to serve a number of purposes, most of which fall into one of five broad categories.

1. *Learning where things are in the library.* Scavenger hunts that focus on locating things are typically designed to expose students to as much of the physical space of the library as possible. In this sense, they are similar to tours. These hunts are based on the assumption that as students seek the items on the assigned list, they must find their way around the library and will thereby become familiar with where things are.

2. *Exposure to critical resources and services.* Scavenger hunts may also be designed to expose students to library resources and services that will be useful in the current course and beyond. Encyclopedias, the reference collection and staff, and similar universally helpful items are typically seen on this type of scavenger hunt.

3. *Exposure to course- or assignment-specific resources and services.* Whereas the preceding kind of scavenger hunt introduces students to a broad cross section of relevant resources and services, another sort of scavenger hunt revolves around a specific assignment or course. A scavenger hunt for a course on Shakespeare, for example, would focus on resources related to the study of Shakespeare and his works.

4. *Introduction of key personnel.* Many scavenger hunts require that students speak with a specific individual within the library to learn about a specific service or resource. The intent of such activities is for students to gain firsthand knowledge from an expert. Many times that person will be a reference librarian. This introduces students to a person who can help them with assignments in the future.

5. *Reverse hunts.* A reverse scavenger hunt is also designed to expose students to resources and services, but it takes a reverse approach. Students are given a series of questions and, usually, a list of resources that contain the answers. The idea is that as students examine the sources to find the answers, they will come to know the function and value of each source.

A number of criteria are used to create the list of items for a scavenger hunt. The academic level of the students is central. For example, the needs of first-year students will typically be far different from the needs of graduate students. Other common criteria for compiling a list relate to the requirements of a specific assignment, the content of a particular course or topic, and the needs of a specific discipline. Lists of seminal works and resources and services of interest to the faculty member are also common.

WHAT *NOT* TO DO

A scavenger hunt is arguably the least effective of all assignments involving the library. This is not to say that slightly effective scavenger hunts cannot be developed. However, even the best are still problematic. Consequently, as with other assignments, the drawbacks should be carefully weighed against the hoped-for benefits. The remainder of this chapter focuses on some of the many problems and concerns associated with scavenger hunts. Although suggestions for overcoming these challenges are included, faculty should be strongly encouraged to consider developing a different kind of assignment.

One of the most common forms of scavenger hunt is designed to serve as a tour. This type of scavenger hunt is typically seen in freshman introductory courses (e.g., English 101) that teach fundamental research and expository writing skills. Various orientation activities and first-year experience classes designed to develop skills for college success also sometimes employ this sort of activity as a way of introducing students to the physical space of the library. Consider the following excerpt from a sample assignment:

> This scavenger hunt is an extra-credit assignment. To complete it, you will need to go through the entire library. In doing so, you will become familiar with key services and resources the library has to offer. If you wish to receive credit, your results must be turned in by the start of the next class.
> 1. What is the number of the library director's office?
> 2. Are there private study rooms available to students?
> 3. Using microfilm, locate and print out the front page of a newspaper that was published on the day of your birth.
> 4. What is the name of the person in charge of interlibrary loan?
> 5. Locate the head reference librarian and have that person sign this sheet to show that the two of you have spoken about the purpose of the reference collection and reference librarians.

Even in such a short excerpt, several shortcomings are readily apparent.

- Is the correct answer to question 1 an office number or a telephone number?

- Microfilm is a great resource for accessing and retrieving older information. Given that most students' birth dates will be relatively recent, question 3 doesn't really showcase the value of microfilm. It would be more effective to ask students to find content from a much earlier date.

- Just asking for the name of a person, as in question 4, doesn't require students to actually locate that person or to demonstrate that they understand the service for which that person is responsible.

Problems

Among the many problems that quickly emerge from the sample assignment are the following:

The purpose of the assignment is unclear. The combination of questions asking students for specific information (e.g., question 4) and questions requiring students to perform some procedure to obtain the required information (e.g., question 3) makes it difficult for students to determine the purpose of the assignment. Is the goal to learn about the location of resources and services in the library, to discover how to use them, or some combination of the two? Making this an optional rather than a required assignment adds to the confusion. Some students, not knowing whether to take the assignment seriously, will decide not to complete it. As a result, if the assignment is indeed successful in introducing students to the library, only those students who complete it will benefit.

How are answers to be evaluated? Students need to know the grading criteria for an assignment. For example, will the instructor accept just one way of answering question 5? If so, what if a student supplies a different answer that is nonetheless correct? Furthermore, is this an all-or-nothing assignment? That is, say the entire exercise consists of twenty questions. Will students who manage to answer only some of the questions be eligible to receive a grade? Or will grades be given only to students who answer all questions?

Students are likely to perceive the assignment as insignificant. The fact that the assignment is extra credit immediately gives the impression that it's superfluous, that it's not important enough to be a required assignment. The content may, in turn, be seen as arbitrary or trivial, which diminishes or even eliminates the significance of the information it was intended to illustrate.

ISSUES/CONCERNS
Unstated or Unclear Purpose

One of the primary reasons a scavenger hunt is ineffective is that it lacks a clear purpose. It's difficult to determine why some faculty members prefer to send students to the library for a scavenger hunt rather than request a tour.

When a scavenger hunt is used as a means of exposing students to library resources and services and their use, the size of the library is irrelevant. Whether a library is big or small, it is impossible to create a scavenger hunt that effectively accomplishes such a broad purpose. Expecting students to figure out how to use a resource or service once they find it is naive at best. In many cases, librarians must provide instruction and guidance, which can be time-consuming for both the student and the librarian. It is more effective and a far better use of time and resources to schedule classes in which groups of students receive instruction at the same time.

In addition, scavenger hunts tend to overlook one of the greatest strengths of a library—the logical, organized way in which its resources and services are arranged and operate. When students are sent to randomly scour the library, they rarely see or come to understand this organizational structure and how it can be helpful to them. In fact, quite the opposite may occur, and the scavenger hunt may actually reinforce the idea that libraries are exasperating and difficult to navigate.

The scavenger lists themselves are another source of confusion. Most resemble shopping lists in that they lack a common theme or purpose. Although the items are probably significant and chosen with good intentions, faculty members should not assume that students unfamiliar with libraries or the research process can independently make connections between the items they seek and how those items work together. On the other hand, focusing on only one type of item or service (e.g., the reference collection) may be self-defeating as well in that students won't gain exposure to other equally valuable services and resources.

Suggestions

- If the purpose of a scavenger hunt is merely to expose students to the physical locations of things in the library, suggest a tour or give students a map.
- Encourage faculty to tie their scavenger hunts in with a subsequent assignment and to include items on the list that will help students complete that assignment. Although this won't ensure that students know what the items are or how to use them, it will at least give them a starting point for the work they'll do later.
- Help instructors consider the order of the items on their lists. Sequence the items so that students can find them without a lot of backtracking, or present them in the order in which they might be used for an assignment. This helps to eliminate some of the randomness as long as students complete the tasks in order.

Lack of or Ambiguous Relevance

The possibility that students will perceive a scavenger hunt as busywork should be a key concern. Scavenger hunts are often stand-alone, one-shot activities. Because little follow-up or additional context is provided in the class, they are often viewed as just another assignment to complete rather than something inherently valuable.

Contributing to this problem is the idea that one size fits all. Every student has different needs, expectations, and experiences in using a library. As a result, scavenger hunts may be either too general or too specific to be useful for all students.

Some instructors will knowingly include hard-to-find items in a scavenger hunt. This raises even more doubts about the activity's relevance. Other instructors will include a hard-to-find item innocently because they believe the resource is useful. However, given that most scavenger hunts are distributed to freshmen, faculty members should be helped to understand that many students may not be ready to understand the value of the resources they worked so hard to find.

Many times, sending students in search of obscure resources is little more than an attempt to infuse some sort of rigor into the assignment. Some faculty members see a direct relationship between the difficulty of finding a resource and its value. That is, the harder an item is to find, the more useful it must be, and, consequently, the larger the number of such items included in a scavenger hunt, the more valuable the activity must be. The fact that a faculty member feels the need to "infuse rigor" is a strong indication that the assignment probably isn't strong enough to stand on its own in the first place. Some students may benefit from exposure to arcane resources, but others may conclude that the library has a lot of difficult-to-find, often irrelevant materials they'll never use or see once the assignment is completed.

Suggestions

- Work with faculty members to link scavenger hunts with subsequent class assignments or discussion topics.
- Suggest to faculty members that instead of having students just find items on a list, it can be more productive to ask them to write one or two paragraphs about how a resource or service might be useful to them, what questions they might want to ask about it, and so on. This will help students think about library resources and services in personal terms and reveal questions that need to be discussed in class.
- Develop scavenger hunts with different items and emphases to meet the needs of specific courses or groups of students.

Missing Resources

Perhaps the biggest logistical problem students face when completing a scavenger hunt is missing resources. Resources may be missing for a number of reasons. No library could ever possibly have every resource. Even classics that every library should have may not be in the collection. Others may not yet be cataloged, shelved, or otherwise available for use.

Along the same lines, more and more resources are becoming available electronically. Increasingly, libraries are canceling print subscriptions in favor of more accessible electronic versions. Students may not know where to find such electronic resources or how to access them effectively. When libraries switch to electronic versions, they may or may not keep the equivalent printed resources in the collection. Similarly, a printed resource (e.g., *Readers' Guide*) may be replaced with an electronic resource with the same name or with a different product entirely (e.g., Academic Search Premiere). Either way, a faculty member may still want students to use the printed version or may not be aware that a (current) printed version is no longer available.

Sometimes items are truly missing. The more students assigned to complete the same scavenger hunt, the more missing items will become an issue. In the best-case scenario, books may not be lost but merely misshelved or on a cart somewhere waiting to be shelved. In a worst-case scenario, though, the first student to find an item may purposely sign it out, hide it, or damage it to prevent other students from properly completing the assignment.

When a required item is missing, regardless of why, it is often unclear if alternative versions or editions are acceptable. It really depends on the purpose of the assignment. If the goal of a hunt is to expose students to resources, earlier editions would probably be fine. For example, if the current edition of an almanac is missing, an earlier edition would probably be acceptable. However, if the purpose is to expose students to a particular edition for a particular reason, an earlier edition would not do. Style manuals are a good example. There were many significant changes between the fifth and sixth editions of the *Publication Manual of the APA*. Using the fourth edition to write a paper would probably not be acceptable. A related concern is relevance. Sometimes when students are asked to find a specific item, it's not clear if the focus should be on the item or its content. For example, students may be asked to find a dictionary on a specific topic, such as solar energy. However, even if such a dictionary exists, a library may not have a copy. Students may then be forced to decide if their having looked for the dictionary on solar energy will suffice or if their instructor expects them to examine a more general science dictionary for information on solar energy.

Having students retrieve actual items is a problem in many ways. First and foremost, "The early bird gets the worm." As noted above, a student may sign out an item or purposely cause it to become "lost." Or after finding an item, a student may not place it back in its proper spot or may put it on a shelving cart. Depending on staff availability, the item may sit on the cart for several days until it is located and reshelved. In addition, it takes considerable staff time to reshelve books, and reshelving the same ones every day may become annoying. A large number of students working on the same assignment at the same time or having a relatively small window during which the scavenger hunt can be completed only exacerbates these problems.

Suggestions

- Ask faculty members to avoid requiring students to bring items to class or otherwise remove them from the shelves. Recommend that they instead instruct students to indicate exactly where each item can be found and how they found it. Merely providing a book's call number doesn't prove that students know how or where to find the book.
- Whenever possible, review each scavenger hunt before it is distributed to make sure that all the items are available in the collection and accessible to students.
- Strongly encourage faculty members to place commonly used items on reserve so that they will not be signed out or otherwise unavailable during a scavenger hunt.
- Help faculty members to update assignments as needed to reflect current versions of items and to clarify whether earlier editions and electronic versions are acceptable.

Who Actually Does the Work

Another key logistical concern is who actually completes the assignment. When students all have the same list of items to find, some will quickly band together and divvy up the work. For example, instead of each student finding all fifteen items on a list, five students might team up to find three items each and then share their answers. Obviously, in this scenario students are getting a piecemeal understanding of the library.

Also, some students may complete their scavenger hunts by finding someone in the library who's willing to help. The students present their lists to the person, who then answers their questions. Once one student finds such a person, word is likely to spread, and others will discover the person on their own. In the process, students learn who will help them but don't learn much about how to help themselves. The situation reinforces a student's sense of helplessness and creates dependency on the library staff.

From the library's point of view, students are placing an unnecessary burden on the library staff. In a best-case scenario, staff members are contacted ahead of time to ensure that they're willing to help, students arrive in small groups, and the assignment is distributed in only one course per term. Unfortunately, the reality is often that staff members aren't contacted in advance to determine if they're willing and available to help; students arrive one at a time and must be given individual attention, which consumes huge amounts of time; and the assignment is distributed to multiple sections of multiple courses. Making matters worse is the number of students who will wait until the last minute to complete the assignment.

Some faculty members may think they can reduce the burden by telling students not to ask for help. But in the long run, this makes a bad situation even worse in that it doesn't help students understand the role of librarians or how they can help down the road. It instead establishes an unnecessary and damaging barrier to communication.

Suggestions

- When working with faculty members, emphasize that they should never tell students not to ask a librarian for help.
- If you're not willing to take on the role of contact person during a scavenger hunt, determine which librarians are willing and able to help with this assignment. At the very least, they should know the number of students involved, the number of questions they can anticipate, and the amount of time and depth they should give to their answers.
- Encourage instructors to develop and distribute a variety of scavenger lists within each section of a course. This means more work for both faculty members and library staff but helps reduce students' ability to employ a divide-and-conquer approach.

Perceived Value of Items on the List

Students are likely to inflate the importance of the items on the list for a scavenger hunt. Because their instructor thinks an item is significant enough to be included on the list, students may perceive it to have inherent value. Worse, some students may come to believe that the items on the list are the only important resources in the library.

The reverse is also true. Because not every important item can be included on the list, some students may never discover key services and resources. Some may even assume that items omitted from the list are not important or of value to them.

This can be particularly problematic with scavenger hunts used as tours. Some items on the list may have been included merely as a means of getting students from one course-related point to another. However, students may not realize that those items are just signs along the road rather than important destinations in their own right.

Suggestion

■ If instructors have not already done so, make sure students understand that the list merely presents a cross section of library resources and is in no way intended to be exhaustive. Furthermore, students should not assume that the items on the list are the only useful resources to be found in the library or that items omitted from the list are not important. You or the faculty members involved or both need to provide follow-up through additional assignments and user education.

Product versus Process

When faculty members devise scavenger hunts, they often focus on product, not process. That is, they require students to locate or retrieve an item but pay little attention to how students do so. As a result, students are unlikely to analyze the search process and learn how to do an effective search on their own. This is another situation that creates unnecessary dependence on the library staff. Focusing on product over process fails to teach students what a resource or service is, how to use it, and when it might be useful to them.

Underlying this sort of scavenger hunt are a number of assumptions. Let's say, for example, that students are to locate a gazetteer and write down its call number. A key assumption is that students will know which resource to use (i.e., the online public access catalog [OPAC]), how to access this resource, and how to use it to find a gazetteer. Because the call number will appear in the item's record, students do not need to locate the actual book. This defeats at least part of the assignment's purpose of having students find the item. Moreover, it's not safe to assume that just because students have an item's call number they will be able to locate the item in the future or that they will know what a gazetteer is and how one might be used.

At the most basic level is the mistaken assumption that students will actually do all of the expected work in the first place. For example, students in the same class working on the same assignment may find the required gazetteer lying on a table or shelving cart instead of in its usual location. And, in many instances, students will simply request the gazetteer from a librarian, who will produce it without questioning why it's needed.

Suggestions

- Work with faculty to develop scavenger hunts that focus on the process, not the product. Encourage them to require that students detail how they found each item. At the very least, students should be asked to discuss the people they spoke with, the resources they used to locate each item, and the specific location of each shelved item.
- Suggest that students be asked to provide a brief description of each required resource or service and to explain how it might be useful to them—now or in the future.

Importance of the Library

Some instructors who assign scavenger hunts assume that because such activities require a trip to the library, students will automatically understand that knowing about the library is important. Others, as mentioned earlier, may allow students to do scavenger hunts for extra credit even though such an approach may trivialize the library and lead students to believe that library skills are not important enough to merit the entire class's attention. That notion will be reinforced if after a scavenger hunt there is little or no follow-up discussion or activity in class.

Suggestions

- Help faculty members understand why a scavenger hunt should not be used as an extra-credit assignment.
- Persuade instructors to discuss what students learned from the scavenger hunt in class. When going over common problems that students encountered, faculty should emphasize the importance of the library and how the ability to access its resources and services can save time, improve grades, and more.

One-on-One Contact

In general, the interpersonal dynamic is often overlooked in a scavenger hunt. Females from patriarchal societies, for example, may be culturally conditioned not to ask males questions. Males from some cultures may feel it is not appropriate for them to ask a female for assistance. Wheelchair-bound students may not be able to reach required items. These sorts of issues may not be easily overcome. Still, faculty members should be made aware of them and attempt to make as many reasonable accommodations as possible.

In spite of or because of such concerns, instructors will sometimes require students to speak with a specific person in the library. At first glance, requiring contact with a specific person appears to have merit. To learn about a particular resource or service, it makes sense for students to speak with the person who knows the most about it. Doing so also gives students a familiar face to look for when they come to the library.

Sometimes, though, an instructor may not be aware of the most appropriate person to contact. Other times, the recommended person may merely be a personal acquaintance of the faculty member and may or may not be the best person to advise students.

In addition, as in any other place of employment, there are friendly, helpful people in the library and there are those who aren't. Some instructors may fail to alert their recommended contacts that students may be seeking them out. And it can't be assumed that everyone will be available and willing to drop everything to spend time with students. Not surprisingly, when a designated person is not available or students perceive that they're not being given the attention they expect, the situation may quickly become awkward and frustrating.

Even when the recommended person is available and willing to help, what to say or do with the students may not be clear. Moreover, the time commitment may be daunting. If a class has twenty-five students, spending just five minutes per student would consume more than two hours of the person's time. Most deans and department heads are unlikely to look favorably on this sort of scenario. In addition, this approach may mislead students into thinking that the recommended person is the only one who can help with a particular type of question when, in fact, many people may be able to provide assistance.

When instructors require students to meet with a library staff member, whether identified by name or not, they often require a signature from that person. This is viewed as a way of ensuring that students fulfilled the assignment. However, instructors are not only unlikely to have every current library staff member's signature on file but equally unlikely to review each signature for authenticity. Moreover, due to other obligations and commitments, some library staff members may sign their names without spending time with students. As a result, even though students may have the required signature, they won't know anything about the person they were asked to contact or that person's role in the library.

Suggestions

- Urge faculty members to speak with a librarian to determine the best way to arrange for students to meet with library staff. The number and availability of staff as well as staffing patterns will differ from one library to another. Depending on circumstances, requiring students to speak with a reference librarian instead of a specific individual might be advisable. Another approach may be to have a library staff member speak with the entire class at one time.
- Requiring students to obtain a signature is cumbersome, impractical, and unreliable. If an instructor insists that students must speak with someone in person, suggest that students be asked to write a paragraph or two summarizing what they learned about the services for which that individual is responsible.
- Emphasize the importance of finding the right person with whom to speak. This is not just a good library lesson, it's a good life lesson as well.

Faculty Agenda

Particularly in light of all of the new information resources and access points that have emerged over the past decade or so, some instructors are not comfortable with today's modern library. In response, some instructors may assign a scavenger hunt as a way of improving their own knowledge about new resources and services. By reading what students turn in, the instructors are able to learn as well.

Suggestion

- A better way to familiarize faculty members with the library is to hold one-on-one meetings to provide information on new resources and services and to discuss how the library can best meet their individual needs. Cordially invite them to the library and offer to show them the areas that interest them the most.

Requiring an Actual Item or Use of Service

Requiring students to retrieve an item and bring it to class should be strongly discouraged, particularly for irreplaceable, one-of-a-kind resources (e.g., an autographed copy of a book of Robert Frost's poetry). If there is only one copy of an item, the first student to find it will be the only one able to bring it to class. Beyond that, though, every item brought to class is an item that will take staff time to sign out and eventually reshelve. Moreover, if students are asked to bring a newspaper or magazine article back to class, they may actually rip it out of its original source.

Requiring the use of a service should also be discouraged. It is admirable to have students learn about the function and value of interlibrary loan. But having every student in a class submit a request for a book or article wastes considerable time and money on something that will probably never be read or used.

Suggestions

- Strongly dissuade faculty members from requiring students to retrieve items and bring them to class. Having students provide a title, call number, and location is generally sufficient for a book. For an article, students might submit a photocopy of the first page or of the cover of the issue in which the article appeared. However, as more and more articles become available electronically, providing proof that they were found is increasingly problematic, except for significantly older items.
- Explain to faculty why students should not be asked to use services that they don't really need. Students can complete a request form (e.g., for an interlibrary loan) and bring it to class without actually submitting the form for processing. When a service has no request form, have students write one or two paragraphs about the service and how and when it would be used.

DOS AND DON'TS

"Good scavenger hunt" is an oxymoron. As noted throughout this chapter, there are a number of problems associated with having students complete a scavenger hunt. The drawbacks typically far outweigh any possible benefits that might be achieved. For that reason, instructors should be strongly discouraged from using scavenger hunts as an instructional tool.

Consider sharing the dos and don'ts below with individuals who insist on assigning scavenger hunts. The list is in no way comprehensive. Although following the suggestions will help instructors create better scavenger hunts, it is highly unlikely that such activities—no matter how well designed and administered—will yield the hoped-for results.

DO	DON'T
Have a clear purpose in mind.	Do NOT attempt to use a scavenger hunt as both a tour and a way to familiarize students with library resources and services.
Tie the hunt in to a primary topic of the course or a subsequent assignment.	
Be specific about the resources you wish students to find and be sure they exist in the library as indicated in the assignment.	Do NOT assign a scavenger hunt without some sort of context.
To discourage group work, develop multiple versions of a scavenger hunt, with each calling for different items.	Do NOT distribute the assignment without first verifying that the items you've listed are actually available and accessible to students.
Only include items relevant to the purpose of the assignment.	Do NOT distribute the exact same scavenger hunt to a class or classes.
To help students learn how to find things on their own and to recognize their value or usefulness, focus on the process of finding the items rather than on the items themselves.	Do NOT create an arbitrary list of items and resources.
	Do NOT expect students to know how to use the resources that will help them find the required items.
Stress the importance of the library during both the distribution of the assignment and the follow-up discussion.	Do NOT expect a single assignment to teach students to recognize the usefulness of the library or the items on the scavenger list.
If students are expected to seek out someone specific in the library, contact the person beforehand to get her permission and to explain her intended role in the assignment.	Do NOT ask students to meet one-on-one with a specific person in the library or require that they acquire that person's signature.
Schedule a one-on-one session with a librarian if you're interested in learning about library resources and services.	

(cont.)

DO	DON'T
Have students discuss library processes rather than actually perform the processes.	Do NOT include hard-to-find or dated materials that students will be unlikely to use now or in the future.
Place on reserve items that will be hard to access or that the entire class will be using.	Do NOT require students to find items that necessitate the use of other resources (e.g., catalog, index).
Provide follow-up activities and discussion to build on what students learned and to address problems that they encountered.	

PART V CROSSING THE BRIDGE
Working with Faculty-Developed Library Assignments

ELEVEN IN THE CLASSROOM

DESCRIPTION

At institutions where information literacy is not fully integrated into the curriculum, instruction in the use of library resources and services is typically initiated by a faculty member teaching a course involving the library. A faculty member teaching a course on Shakespeare, for example, may be having her students write a paper on one of the author's plays. At some point in the term, she would seek out a librarian who could inform students about the library's Shakespeare resources (e.g., books, videos) and provide instruction in the use of various information tools (e.g., databases, Web) that students might use to find additional information. For this reason, instruction usually takes place in a fifty-minute or seventy-five-minute time frame—the typical length of most undergraduate class periods.

The instruction that's provided may take many forms. In an ideal situation, the librarian would work with the faculty member beforehand to create an effective assignment. Often, though, the faculty member will have already distributed the assignment, and the librarian will need to develop instruction accordingly. In most instances, the instruction will be geared to a particular assignment or aspects of an assignment. However, the instructor may simply want her students to know how to access and use a particular resource for subsequent assignments, or she may want a more general discussion about evaluating websites. The number of possible scenarios is virtually limitless.

THE BENEFITS

There are many benefits to be derived from providing classroom instruction to students. Obviously, at the very least, students gain a clearer idea of what resources to use and how to use them to retrieve the information they need to complete their assignments. Some of the many other benefits include enabling librarians to

- reach more students more quickly with the information they need to complete their assignments

- be more aware of faculty expectations with regard to how students are to complete their assignments

- address specific problems and concerns that have emerged in the past

- alert students to potential problems and common pitfalls before they happen

- provide students and faculty alike with information about changes to resources and services

- develop their working relationship with the faculty member and department

- increase their approachability factor

THE ANATOMY OF INSTRUCTION

Appendix C provides an overview of the history of different types of instruction involving the library. Library orientation is at the low end. It tends to focus on the mere location of things and is typically evidenced by tours and scavenger hunts. Information literacy instruction, on the other hand, is at the high end and typically involves the entire campus playing a part in the provision of "information education." Although a curriculum-wide information literacy program is clearly the goal for many institutions, most information instruction currently falls somewhere between the two ends of the spectrum.

At many institutions, traditional bibliographic instruction or library instruction continues to form the core of instruction offered by librarians. The provision of such instruction typically progresses through a series of five steps.

Step 1: Need for instruction identified. Awareness of a need for instruction may emerge in any number of ways, but three are especially common:

- Faculty members or librarians identify courses incorporating a research component.

- Librarians notice consistent and persistent problems when working with students completing their assignments.

- Faculty members recognize deficiencies in students' research skills or have assignment-specific needs they wish to have addressed by a librarian.

Step 2: Relevant strategies discussed. The librarian meets with the faculty member to discuss students' specific instructional needs and how they could be best addressed.

- The librarian and the faculty member examine the assignment.

- The two discuss expectations and limitations of library instruction.

- The librarian and the instructor work together to establish the format and content of the instruction session.

Step 3: Instruction session scheduled. Once the content and structure of the instruction session are established, a mutually convenient time, date, and place for instruction are determined.

- The amount of time between the scheduling of the class and the class itself will vary. However, at least a week is recommended so that the librarian will have time to prepare and the faculty member will have time to announce the instruction session to the students.

- A librarian who will go to the classroom to provide instruction needs to visit the room beforehand to ensure that it has all of the software, hardware, equipment, and supplies needed to hold the class.

- A librarian who will use a room in the library to provide instruction needs to ensure that there are enough seats, computers (if available), and other equipment and supplies needed to hold the class.

Step 4: Instruction session held. A sample format for a typical one-shot instruction session is presented at the end of this chapter.

Step 5: Evaluation conducted. An evaluation of the librarian's presentation may take the form of an in-class assessment or a follow-up with the faculty member after students have completed the assignment. Evaluation typically focuses on the presentation style and abilities of the librarian, the content of the instruction, or some combination of both. Narrative responses are usually the most useful but take time to compose and write. Yes/no and scaled answers are quicker to generate but often lack any meaningful context. For example, in response to the same question, one student's answer of 2 might mean the same as another student's 4. Questions to consider asking in the evaluation of a librarian's presentation include the following:

- Did instruction address the needs originally identified?

- Which elements needed more emphasis?

- Which elements needed less emphasis?
- Which topics were the most useful?
- Which topics were the least useful?
- What wasn't discussed that should have been?

THE CHALLENGES
Instruction Is Scheduled without a Clear Assignment or List of Expectations

When a faculty member requests library instruction without specifying an assignment or set of expectations, it is difficult to develop a meaningful and relevant presentation. If there is no context for the presentation or if there is no follow-up activity (e.g., a graded quiz), students will quickly perceive library instruction as little more than busywork, something that has to be endured to complete the course. In turn, they are likely to promptly forget what they've learned, if they learn anything at all. Many librarians are reluctant to deny a request for instruction, but to ensure the most effective use of everyone's time, it is best to turn down instructors who don't provide adequate background information.

Suggestion
- Never schedule instruction before receiving a copy of the assignment or a list of clearly defined expectations and topics to be addressed.

Due to Limited Class Time, Key Content Must Be Sacrificed

Because it's impossible to address every relevant topic and answer every question in a single fifty-minute time period, a key challenge is deciding what content to present. A conscious decision has to be made about whether a few topics should be covered well or many topics should be touched on lightly. The librarian must also decide how much time to devote to hands-on activities, students' questions, accommodating different learning styles, and related issues (e.g., remote access). Hands-on activities, for example, are a great way to learn. Unfortunately, even in small classes, time for hands-on activities may not be practical or even available.

Suggestions
- Use the assignment to focus the content of the instruction.
- Depending on the skill levels of students, focus first on broader, more universal issues and topics (e.g., subject vs. keyword searching).
- Develop an instructional menu that lets faculty know what instruction can be provided and a rough estimate of the minimum amount of class time needed for each topic. The instructor can then pick and choose the topics to be covered in the time available.

■ Encourage faculty to pair one classroom instruction session with a hands-on working day in the library during which you or another librarian will work with students one-on-one to address specific issues.

Students Have Varied Skills and Assignment Needs

As noted earlier, students may have good computer skills or good research skills. But it is a rare student who possesses both. Moreover, faculty members cannot rely on other courses or other departments to have given students the skills they need to complete their current assignment. At best, most students have a piecemeal set of skills and abilities that may or may not be adequate to complete the assignment successfully. Teaching to such a varied audience is difficult because you risk giving a presentation that is either too advanced or too rudimentary for a significant portion of students.

Suggestions

■ Suggest the faculty member conduct a basic needs assessment of students in the class prior to the instruction session as a way to focus instruction where needed and refrain from talking about topics that aren't as urgent.
■ Focus on general, conceptual sorts of things in class and encourage students to meet with you one-on-one to address specific issues or needs they might have.
■ Provide handouts, follow-up activities, tutorials, and so on that students can examine and work through at their own pace.

Adequate Attention Must Be Given to Technology

Many instruction sessions typically focus on how to access and use a given resource. However, because of the growing interdependence of information and technology, it would be remiss not to incorporate at least a cursory discussion of technology into every instruction session. Determining how much or how little, though, is the problem. For example, given the preponderance of resources now available to off-site users, most librarians probably feel comfortable mentioning how to access resources from home as well as some of the technology-related problems home access might entail. And yet, any time spent on off-site access means less time for other topics.

Suggestion

■ Develop a list of commonly experienced technical problems and their solutions and make it available to students via a web page or handout.

TIPS FOR SUCCESS

Specify that the earliest possible date for instruction will be at least one week after the librarian has received a copy of an assignment or a list of expectations. Some faculty are notorious for calling the library only one or two days before their preferred date of instruction. This is inconsiderate of the faculty member, but it reflects even more negatively on any librarian who would agree to the request. Giving such short notice implies that librarians have nothing better to do or that their time is somehow less valuable than that of a faculty member. It also suggests to students that library instruction isn't important enough to schedule in advance. When done at the last minute like this, the resulting instruction more closely resembles babysitting than sound pedagogy. Requiring a week's notice gives the librarian a chance to prepare a quality, focused presentation and reinforces mutual respect and professionalism.

Approachable librarians are key to student success with library-related assignments. Simply put, if students don't feel comfortable asking for assistance, they won't. Avoiding the librarian may result in considerable amounts of wasted time, frustration, and inefficient use of resources. The person who presents library instruction will typically be the primary person students seek out when they need help. Taking time during a presentation to let students know that you expect them to contact you and to identify the best times and ways of doing so will go a long way in creating a win-win environment for all involved.

Use your time wisely and make the assignment the focal point of your classroom time. There is no doubt that the library has many resources with features and functions that are invaluable to researchers. However, spending all three hours of a graduate course talking about the bells and whistles of your OPAC is generally not the best use of time. Such lengthy digressions not only take valuable time away from the discussion of other resources and services but also increase the risk of information overload. Presentation of more than just the basics of any new topic may quickly become confusing. Focusing on the assignment and showing students how they can use your information to complete the assignment more effectively and efficiently leads to a much more practical and meaningful (and well-received) presentation.

Be prepared with examples to ensure that key points are demonstrated properly. Asking the professor for topics that students might be working on will help you to develop relevant examples. Some librarians like to solicit students' input about their topics during the class. Such an activity needs to be carefully controlled because pursuing a topic that is obscure or nonresearchable may waste valuable class time and cause unnecessary confusion. It may also make the librarian appear disorganized (at best) or incompetent (when results aren't found).

Share course assignments with your colleagues. Sharing assignments with your colleagues helps to improve the level of service they are able to provide. It also prepares them for the questions they'll face when on duty at the reference desk and helps everyone feel more involved. You might even consider attaching your lecture notes so that your colleagues will know what you discussed in class, what obstacles you foresee, and so on. If you post the assignments electronically, be sure your colleagues are the only ones who have access or that you've removed any identifying information. Leaving a faculty member's name on a poorly created assignment can be embarrassing, may result in an uncomfortable confrontation, and is certain to jeopardize any future collaboration on assignments and instruction. It's also crucial to ensure that students can't access the assignments.

Meet with the faculty member before and after you've given instruction. As has been noted throughout this book, it is important to meet with faculty members before an assignment is distributed. This is especially true before an instruction session to help ensure that the examples shown in class are relevant, that possible obstacles students might encounter are addressed, and that the overall presentation matches the needs of the class and their instructor.

It is equally important to meet with faculty members after the instruction session has been held. This provides an opportunity to determine if the instruction was effective, if it met the students' and instructor's needs, if students' potential problems with the assignment were sufficiently addressed, and so on. Decisions and recommendations can then be made about future iterations of the assignment and the corresponding instruction.

DOS AND DON'TS

The following are just a few of the ways in which instruction sessions can be improved:

DO	DON'T
Gear instruction to the specific needs of the students in the context of their assignment.	Do not provide instruction that's not directed to a specific assignment.
Focus on the resource features and functions that are most appropriate to the assignment.	Do not talk about all the impressive things a resource does unless they're relevant to the assignment.
Infuse your personality into the presentation.	Do not lose yourself or be intimidated.
Decide ahead of time how much time and attention to devote to each topic.	Do not spend an entire class period talking about one resource or group of features, unless that's what the instructor requested.
Come to class with examples (preferably supplied or suggested by the instructor) that demonstrate key features and functions as they relate to the assignment or area of study.	Do not spontaneously solicit problems or examples from the students.

ONE-SHOT INSTRUCTION SESSION: SAMPLE FORMAT

As noted earlier, for a variety of reasons, librarians are often given only a single class period in which to make a presentation. That's why such sessions are often referred to as one-shot instruction. Some librarians opt for more hands-on activity and less discussion. Others prefer to show a variety of resources without going into too much detail. Still others focus on a small number of topics and go into greater detail. What's most effective depends on what's expected. Again, whatever instruction is provided should relate to the specific assignment on which the students are working.

Table 11.1 provides a framework for a generic instruction session that covers the basics of how to look for books and articles but not much more. It provides enough information to get most students started but not so much that they become overwhelmed, confused, or intimidated. The content focuses on broad functions and concepts (e.g., keyword vs. subject searching) rather than specific features and keystrokes.

TABLE 11.1   SAMPLE FRAMEWORK FOR A FIFTY-FIVE-MINUTE INSTRUCTION SESSION

STAGE	DURATION	ACTIVITY
Before class	Varies	Develop assignment with faculty member
Stage 1	5 minutes	Introduce self and purpose/context of presentation; emphasize importance of asking for help
Stage 2	10 minutes	Finding books—introduce catalog and basic search using keywords
Stage 3	20 minutes	Finding articles—introduce one relevant database but indicate other possibilities
Stage 4	10 minutes	Discuss computing and other nonresearch difficulties students may face
Stage 5	10 minutes	Closure, questions and answers
After class	Varies	Make yourself available to students immediately after class; contact professor with follow-up questions/observations; distribute handout to colleagues who might work with students, alerting them to specific needs/expectations

TWELVE IN THE LIBRARY

THE NEED

It would seem reasonable to expect that a student who comes to the library to work on an assignment requiring the use of library resources and services would have a copy of the assignment or at least a clear understanding of what needs to be done. The majority of students do, in fact, arrive with a copy of their assignment, and most librarians can help them to navigate through it without undue difficulty.

Unfortunately, some students arrive with little more than a vague idea of what their assignment is or what they need to do to complete it. When these students seek help, many librarians are uncomfortable providing assistance. They would like to provide good, effective service, but without knowing more about what's needed, they may provide either too much or too little service or service that's completely inappropriate. The ill-prepared student, in turn, might leave the situation with a number of misperceptions about libraries and the assistance librarians are able to provide.

All is not lost, however. Librarians can do a number of things to help students seeking assistance—even those who have forgotten their assignments—now and in the future.

THE CHALLENGES
Students May Have Difficulty Expressing Their Needs

As a rule, librarians are a friendly, approachable bunch. Still, some students are not comfortable asking for assistance. Those feelings may result from any number of factors. For example, some students may have had a bad experience when they asked a librarian for help in the past. Others may feel that asking for help makes them look stupid or unable to help themselves.

Sometimes the reason for a student's lack of self-expression is observable. This can be particularly true of international students who are contending with a language barrier. Even if they're able to communicate in the librarian's language, they may not be familiar with the jargon of libraries or know how to phrase their questions to obtain the information they desire. Students with mental or physical disabilities may be unable to express their needs verbally or in a way that can be understood by the librarian.

Suggestions

- Be patient with students and listen to them carefully.
- Whenever possible, work with faculty members to identify students in their courses who may have special needs and to develop appropriate strategies for assisting them.
- Given that some people may find it easier to write or to type than to speak with a librarian directly, have a notepad handy or suggest students work with you via e-mail or instant messaging to resolve their problems.
- Contact the person responsible for providing services to students with disabilities to determine ways of using aides and assistive technologies to address the needs of students with disabilities; what, if any, accommodations need to be made in library-related assignments and activities; and if other steps can be taken to enhance comfort and learning (e.g., additional time to complete assignments).

Students May Not Know What They Need

Even if students are able to express themselves effectively, they may have only a vague idea of what it is they want or need. For example, a student may merely say that he's working on a paper on a particular topic and needs some help. At first glance, the request may seem straightforward. But the instructor may have imposed additional requirements that are stated only on the original assignment sheet. A requirement to use peer-reviewed sources, for example, is not uncommon. When a student doesn't inform the librarian about all the requirements of an assignment, the librarian can't be expected to provide the best assistance possible.

Suggestion

- Contact the professor, check her web page, and examine your library's assignment notebook for details about the assignment and what's expected.

Students Have Difficulty Generating Effective Search Strategies

There are any number of ways a search for information for an assignment can fail. Sometimes it will be the technology that fails. But often students are at a loss about where to even begin searching. In part, they may not know which resources will provide the information they're seeking. But even if they have selected an appropriate resource, students often have difficulty constructing an effective search strategy. They may find too few or too many sources or fail to find sources that are relevant to their topic or need. Table 12.1 outlines some basic strategies faculty can suggest for overcoming some of the more commonly experienced problems with search strategies.

Students Lack a Clear Topic or One That's Researchable

In completing assignments involving research, students often wag the dog. For any number of reasons, they either don't have a topic in mind when they start their

TABLE 12.1   SOLUTIONS TO COMMON PROBLEMS WITH SEARCH STRATEGIES

PROBLEM	SOLUTION
Terms are too specific	Try alternative terms and ways of saying the same thing (e.g., capital punishment, death penalty). Be aware that some words change over time or with context. *Example:* blacks—1960s, African Americans—today
Incorrect spelling or typing	Always check for misspellings and typographical errors. Alert students that some words have multiple spellings. *Example:* Brazil = Brasil
Inappropriate resource	Suggest using a general resource to broaden a search or browse for ideas; recommend a subject-specific resource to help students quickly focus on more relevant source material.
Too broad or too narrow a topic or strategy	Suggest narrowing or broadening the search using different terms or limits. *Examples:* subject vs. keyword searches; search restricted to peer-reviewed publications
Unclear or unstated perspective	Emphasize the importance of clearly identifying the perspective from which a topic will be explored. *Example:* teacher vs. student views of dress codes
Use of noise words	Words like *of* and *what*—words that don't carry content—should generally not be included in a search unless they're part of a specific phrase. *Examples:* history Paris; *A Tale of Two Cities*

research or they change their topic based on what they find as their research progresses. That is, it is not uncommon to find that, rather than constructing an effective search strategy, students conduct a broad search and find a common thread that then becomes their topic.

Suggestion

- There are any number of strategies you can suggest to faculty or students to assist in generating a good, researchable topic. Some examples include examining the textbook, talking with the instructor or other students about their interests, and selecting a topic related to their major.

Procrastination Limits the Assistance That Can Be Provided

Students have become increasingly accustomed to instant gratification in many areas of their lives. As a result, when completing an assignment they often underestimate the amount of time it will take, particularly if they've never engaged in research before. They often expect research to be a quick and relatively straightforward process. But even in the best of cases, they may encounter technical problems (e.g., resource malfunctions) beyond their control that prevent them from completing their assignments in a timely manner.

Such obstacles and lack of time can dramatically increase the level of stress in students who have procrastinated and create a spike in the amount of frustration and anxiety they may already be feeling about the assignment. In these situations, librarians need to find a balance between their desire to provide good service and the student's need to be done as quickly as possible. Sometimes this may mean telling the student, "I can't do what you want me to do in the time you've given me, but here is what I *can* do." In other cases, there may be nothing the librarian can do. When that happens, it's probably best to say so at the start so that you don't waste your time and the student's or give the impression that you can accomplish the impossible.

Suggestions

- Because individual courses and expectations differ, it's best to work with a faculty member to develop an assignment-completion time frame that suggests the steps students need to go through and realistic approximations of how long each step might take.
- Do as much as you can to provide the best assistance possible in the time you're given.

LIBRARIAN-ASSIGNMENT DYNAMIC REVISITED

Because libraries are all organized differently, an assignment may be administered or otherwise come to the attention of a librarian in many different ways. Three of the most common are

Walk-in. A student approaches a librarian and asks for assistance.

Liaison. The librarian assigned to work with a department becomes aware of an assignment through discussions with the department's faculty members.

Instruction. A librarian is asked to generate instruction geared to a specific assignment or subject area.

As previously observed, when a librarian is helping students complete their assignments, it's not always clear what the students want or what the professor expects. As a result, librarians must often make a leap of faith. They have to use their experience and trust their judgment that the assistance they're providing is both appropriate and worthwhile. To that end, when working with students completing their assignments, librarians may find the acronym LEAP useful:

Listening. Because students may not know or may not be able to clearly articulate what they need, librarians must listen as carefully as possible. Often the things that go unspoken are the most significant.

Evaluation. Whenever possible, examine the assignment to learn the faculty member's specific expectations. If a copy of the assignment isn't available and the professor can't be reached for clarification, decide what seems to be needed and discuss it with the student to ensure you're both thinking similarly.

Action. Based on what you've heard, read, and discussed, act to address the student's needs.

Patience. Be patient. Remember that students come at an assignment from different angles and with different experiences, needs, and expectations. Sometimes the snags you encounter will be attributable to the student, sometimes they will be attributable to the assignment, and sometimes they may even be attributable to the librarian.

WHAT YOU CAN DO

Librarians can do many things to improve interactions with students working on assignments.

Listen to What's Meant, Not Just to What's Said

As noted earlier, students may have difficulty articulating their needs. In such situations, the need for librarians to employ good, effective listening cannot be overstated.

This means not only listening carefully to what's said but also paying attention to nonverbal clues that suggest a student might be dissatisfied. A simple "Is that what you wanted?" or "Come see me if you need more/different information" can go a long way to enhance librarian-student relations, improve the overall quality of the student's work, and create a positive library atmosphere for everyone.

Call Faculty When Necessary to Clarify What's Expected

It isn't necessary to call a faculty member about every assignment-related question that arises. First talk with your fellow librarians to see what, if any, patterns emerge. If several students in the same course have experienced the same problem with an assignment or aren't sure how to interpret something, it's probably a good idea to contact the professor. This approach not only alerts faculty to the existing problems but also may motivate them to change the assignment for future classes.

Share a Copy of Each Assignment with Your Colleagues

Whenever possible, distribute copies of assignments to your colleagues before students start arriving in the library to work on them. One idea is to create an assignment notebook that can be stored in a location to which every librarian has access (e.g., the reference desk). At the very least, the notebook should include copies of syllabi and assignments that have been annotated to highlight specific assignment needs and expectations (e.g., a requirement to use peer-reviewed sources). A list of potential roadblocks students and librarians are likely to encounter and a follow-up list of actual problems encountered may also be useful. These can be used to focus library instruction the next time the assignment is given. Finally, as most assignments are distributed at the same time every semester, arranging the notebook by week can help in the planning process for future assignment, reference, and instruction needs.

Anticipate Who's Going to Need Help and in What Ways

In an ideal world, faculty and librarians would collaborate on every level with every assignment involving the library, from creating the assignment to providing instruction to working with students in the library to following up afterward. Unfortunately, in the real world, that rarely happens. Some faculty will welcome collaboration, but there will always be others who won't schedule instruction or accept suggestions about their assignments. Fortunately, though, the majority of professors fall somewhere in the middle. Although they may not be aware of the problems associated with their assignments, they are often willing to work with a librarian to resolve them if given a chance.

Doing two things can facilitate the process. First, develop a list of courses that require research/library work. Pertinent information can be gathered in a number of ways, such as by contacting department chairs, attending department meetings (especially if the department has a curriculum committee), and participating in campus dialogue about the curriculum.

Second, keep track of which professors send students to the library. When students approach the desk and request assistance, ask them to name their professor and course. One easy way to keep track of such information is to record it in your reference log. Make a distinction between reference questions and instruction questions and add columns for the names of the professor and the course. Note that new course information recorded in the log may be added to the list of courses compiled earlier.

Use your lists to identify and contact faculty members who are scheduled to teach the same courses the following term (or in the future). By contacting instructors before they teach a course again, you will have time to work with them to revise assignments, schedule instruction, and address other issues and needs that might surface.

DOS AND DON'TS

The following are just a few of the many ways in which librarians can help students optimize the time they spend working on assignments in the library:

DO	DON'T
Be patient and listen carefully.	Do not assume students can clearly articulate their needs.
Ask to see a copy of the assignment.	
Work with students to develop a list of resources, terms, strategies, and so on that might be relevant to their topic/need.	Do not expect students to know what they need or want.
	Do not assume students know how to access library resources and construct effective search strategies.
Contact faculty members with questions and observations about their assignments.	Do not neglect problems with assignments when they occur.
Share a copy of each assignment with other librarians.	Do not expect that other librarians will always know how to deal with assignment problems.
Generate a list of courses and professors likely to require research and contact them about scheduling library instruction and discussing their assignments before they're distributed.	Do not wait for questions and problems to arise; try to identify and address potential stumbling blocks in advance.

THIRTEEN SOME FINAL WORDS

NO ONE LIKES TO ADMIT defeat. Because of the strong service-oriented nature of our work, most librarians are committed to going the extra mile to provide whatever assistance is deemed necessary and appropriate. Consequently, we're often reluctant to accept that we were not able to adequately address a patron's needs. It is not uncommon for librarians to equate a failure to help someone with some form of professional failure or personal shortcoming or both.

Unfortunately, some librarians are just not willing or are even unable to acknowledge failure. When pressed, they believe that, given the right amounts of time, resources, and perseverance, they are capable of addressing most problems eventually. Ultimately, statements such as "If only I'd said . . ." or "If only I had more time . . ." often come to reflect denial more than the actual reason behind the failure.

The reality is that everyone fails at some point. Sometimes there's nothing that can be said or done to prevent an assignment from falling short—either now or in the future. Such assignments are usually more the exception than the rule, but they are a reality that all librarians are likely to encounter at some point in their careers. Consequently, librarians must learn to deal effectively with those situations when they occur. Keeping a few simple rules in mind will lessen the frustration of dealing with ineffective assignments.

Be willing to accept and to acknowledge that you might be wrong. Remember that just because you think an assignment is flawed doesn't mean that it is or that the faculty member involved shares your perception. *Never* presume your way is the only way. When speaking with a faculty member, you should never give the impression that you have all of the answers or that your way is inherently better or correct. When you encounter an ineffective assignment, always be willing to consider that perhaps you don't fully understand it or its role in relation to other assignments or to the course as a whole.

Know when to quit. You should always make an effort to speak with faculty members about assignments that fall short. Most professors are open to and welcome such feedback. Sadly, though, some professors will never change their assignments. Although you should still contact them, be watchful for the point of diminishing returns. That is, there comes a time when it's no longer a good use of your time to continue discussions with these faculty members. Accept that things may not change any time soon (if at all) and move on to more productive activities.

Don't beat yourself up after an instruction session. No matter how well you know the assignment or what the professor expects, there will always be something you forgot or didn't have time to demonstrate or discuss. In a fifty-minute class period, given that students have such different skills and needs, there is no way you can anticipate and address every possible question or obstacle they may experience. If you're permitted to provide a follow-up session, that's great. Otherwise, acknowledge the one-shot session for what it is and make the most of the time you're given. For the time being, focus your attention on helping the students when they come to the library and on improving both the assignment and the instruction for next time.

Know your weaknesses. It's impossible to be all things to all people. Some people have more background, skills, or experience in certain areas than other people do. For example, just because you've dealt with an assignment a dozen times in a semester doesn't mean you've done so effectively or in a way that was ultimately beneficial to the student and met faculty expectations. Don't be afraid to refer students to colleagues with more expertise in a particular field or more experience with a particular assignment. Similarly, if you're uncomfortable speaking with a faculty member about a given assignment, there may be another librarian who's willing to do so or feels more comfortable sharing your concerns.

Don't burn your bridges. One ineffective assignment from a professor doesn't mean all subsequent assignments from that person will be problematic as well. Therefore, it is imperative to always, always, always be courteous and respectful and never to personalize your interactions with faculty members. It doesn't help anyone to attack a professor's assignment or teaching style. Remain calm and objective and stay focused on working together to improve the assignment. Acting and speaking in a professional manner will go a long way in establishing a more collaborative working relationship that will facilitate improving the existing assignment and developing subsequent ones.

If you work with students, at some point you're going to encounter assignments that are problematic. It is hoped that the discussions and suggestions presented in this book will help you to cross that bridge when you come to it. In the end, listen well and do the best you can. Think of listening and doing your best as the bricks and mortar of a bridge that will go a long way toward helping you to cement a firm, lasting foundation both with faculty as they develop assignments involving the library and with students as they work on those assignments.

APPENDIX A ASSOCIATION OF COLLEGE AND RESEARCH LIBRARIES INFORMATION LITERACY COMPETENCY STANDARDS FOR HIGHER EDUCATION

PROPOSED AND ADOPTED BY THE ACRL board of directors in 2000, the following standards are taken from the ACRL's "Information Literacy Competency Standards for Higher Education" (Chicago: American Library Association, 2000, 10–16). Available online at www.ala.org/ala/mgrps/divs/acrl/standards/information literacycompetency.cfm.

STANDARD ONE

The information literate student determines the nature and extent of the information needed.

Performance Indicators

1. The information literate student defines and articulates the need for information.

    Outcomes Include

    a. Confers with instructors and participates in class discussions, peer work groups, and electronic discussions to identify a research topic, or other information need

    b. Develops a thesis statement and formulates questions based on the information need

    c. Explores general information sources to increase familiarity with the topic

    d. Defines or modifies the information need to achieve a manageable focus

    e. Identifies key concepts and terms that describe the information need

    f.   Recognizes that existing information can be combined with original thought, experimentation, and/or analysis to produce new information

2.   The information literate student identifies a variety of types and formats of potential sources for information.

Outcomes Include

    a.   Knows how information is formally and informally produced, organized, and disseminated

    b.   Recognizes that knowledge can be organized into disciplines that influence the way information is accessed

    c.   Identifies the value and differences of potential resources in a variety of formats (e.g., multimedia, database, website, data set, audio/visual, book)

    d.   Identifies the purpose and audience of potential resources (e.g., popular vs. scholarly, current vs. historical)

    e.   Differentiates between primary and secondary sources, recognizing how their use and importance vary with each discipline

    f.   Realizes that information may need to be constructed with raw data from primary sources

3.   The information literate student considers the costs and benefits of acquiring the needed information.

Outcomes Include

    a.   Determines the availability of needed information and makes decisions on broadening the information seeking process beyond local resources (e.g., interlibrary loan; using resources at other locations; obtaining images, videos, text, or sound)

    b.   Considers the feasibility of acquiring a new language or skill (e.g., foreign or discipline-based) in order to gather needed information and to understand its context

    c.   Defines a realistic overall plan and time line to acquire the needed information

4.   The information literate student reevaluates the nature and extent of the information need.

Outcomes Include

    a.   Reviews the initial information need to clarify, revise, or refine the question

    b.   Describes criteria used to make information decisions and choices

STANDARD TWO

The information literate student accesses needed information effectively and efficiently.

Performance Indicators

1. The information literate student selects the most appropriate investigative methods or information retrieval systems for accessing the needed information.

   Outcomes Include

   a. Identifies appropriate investigative methods (e.g., laboratory experiment, simulation, fieldwork)

   b. Investigates benefits and applicability of various investigative methods

   c. Investigates the scope, content, and organization of information retrieval systems

   d. Selects efficient and effective approaches for accessing the information needed from the investigative method or information retrieval system

2. The information literate student constructs and implements effectively designed search strategies.

   Outcomes Include

   a. Develops a research plan appropriate to the investigative method

   b. Identifies keywords, synonyms, and related terms for the information needed

   c. Selects controlled vocabulary specific to the discipline or information retrieval source

   d. Constructs a search strategy using appropriate commands for the information retrieval system selected (e.g., Boolean operators, truncation, and proximity for search engines; internal organizers such as indexes for books)

   e. Implements the search strategy in various information retrieval systems using different user interfaces and search engines, with different command languages, protocols, and search parameters

   f. Implements the search using investigative protocols appropriate to the discipline

3. The information literate student retrieves information online or in person using a variety of methods.

   Outcomes Include

   a. Uses various search systems to retrieve information in a variety of formats

   b. Uses various classification schemes and other systems (e.g., call number systems or indexes) to locate information resources within the library or to identify specific sites for physical exploration

    c.   Uses specialized online or in person services available at the institution to retrieve information needed (e.g., interlibrary loan/document delivery, professional associations, institutional research offices, community resources, experts, and practitioners)

    d.   Uses surveys, letters, interviews, and other forms of inquiry to retrieve primary information

4.   The information literate student refines the search strategy if necessary.

Outcomes Include

    a.   Assesses the quantity, quality, and relevance of the search results to determine whether alternative information retrieval systems or investigative methods should be utilized

    b.   Identifies gaps in the information retrieved and determines if the search strategy should be revised

    c.   Repeats the search using the revised strategy as necessary

5.   The information literate student extracts, records, and manages the information and its sources.

Outcomes Include

    a.   Selects among various technologies the most appropriate one for the task of extracting the needed information (e.g., copy/paste software functions, photocopier, scanner, audio/visual equipment, or exploratory instruments)

    b.   Creates a system for organizing the information

    c.   Differentiates between the types of sources cited and understands the elements and correct syntax of a citation for a wide range of resources

    d.   Records all pertinent citation information for future reference

    e.   Uses various technologies to manage the information selected and organized

STANDARD THREE

The information literate student evaluates information and its sources critically and incorporates selected information into his or her knowledge base and value system.

Performance Indicators

1.   The information literate student summarizes the main ideas to be extracted from the information gathered.

Outcomes Include

    a.   Reads the text and selects main ideas

    b.   Restates textual concepts in his/her own words and selects data accurately

    c.   Identifies verbatim material that can be then appropriately quoted

2. The information literate student articulates and applies initial criteria for evaluating both the information and its sources.

    Outcomes Include

    a. Examines and compares information from various sources in order to evaluate reliability, validity, accuracy, authority, timeliness, and point of view or bias

    b. Analyzes the structure and logic of supporting arguments or methods

    c. Recognizes prejudice, deception, or manipulation

    d. Recognizes the cultural, physical, or other context within which the information was created and understands the impact of context on interpreting the information

3. The information literate student synthesizes main ideas to construct new concepts.

    Outcomes Include

    a. Recognizes interrelationships among concepts and combines them into potentially useful primary statements with supporting evidence

    b. Extends initial synthesis, when possible, at a higher level of abstraction to construct new hypotheses that may require additional information

    c. Utilizes computer and other technologies (e.g., spreadsheets, databases, multimedia, and audio/visual equipment) for studying the interaction of ideas and other phenomena

4. The information literate student compares new knowledge with prior knowledge to determine the value added, contradictions, or other unique characteristics of the information.

    Outcomes Include

    a. Determines whether information satisfies the research or other information need

    b. Uses consciously selected criteria to determine whether the information contradicts or verifies information used from other sources

    c. Draws conclusions based upon information gathered

    d. Tests theories with discipline-appropriate techniques (e.g., simulators, experiments)

    e. Determines probable accuracy by questioning the source of the data, the limitations of the information gathering tools or strategies, and the reasonableness of the conclusions

    f. Integrates new information with previous information or knowledge

    g. Selects information that provides evidence for the topic

5. The information literate student determines whether the new knowledge has an impact on the individual's value system and takes steps to reconcile differences.

Outcomes Include

    a.   Investigates differing viewpoints encountered in the literature

    b.   Determines whether to incorporate or reject viewpoints encountered

6.   The information literate student validates understanding and interpretation of the information through discourse with other individuals, subject-area experts, and/or practitioners.

Outcomes Include

    a.   Participates in classroom and other discussions

    b.   Participates in class-sponsored electronic communication forums designed to encourage discourse on the topic (e.g., e-mail, bulletin boards, chat rooms)

    c.   Seeks expert opinion through a variety of mechanisms (e.g., interviews, e-mail, electronic discussion lists)

7.   The information literate student determines whether the initial query should be revised.

Outcomes Include

    a.   Determines if original information need has been satisfied or if additional information is needed

    b.   Reviews search strategy and incorporates additional concepts as necessary

    c.   Reviews information retrieval sources used and expands to include others as needed

STANDARD FOUR

The information literate student, individually or as a member of a group, uses information effectively to accomplish a specific purpose.

Performance Indicators

1.   The information literate student applies new and prior information to the planning and creation of a particular product or performance.

Outcomes Include

    a.   Organizes the content in a manner that supports the purposes and format of the product or performance (e.g., outlines, drafts, storyboards)

    b.   Articulates knowledge and skills transferred from prior experiences to planning and creating the product or performance

    c.   Integrates the new and prior information, including quotations and paraphrasing, in a manner that supports the purposes of the product or performance

    d.   Manipulates digital text, images, and data, as needed, transferring them from their original locations and formats to a new context

2. The information literate student revises the development process for the product or performance.

   Outcomes Include

   a. Maintains a journal or log of activities related to the information seeking, evaluating, and communicating process

   b. Reflects on past successes, failures, and alternative strategies

3. The information literate student communicates the product or performance effectively to others.

   Outcomes Include

   a. Chooses a communication medium and format that best supports the purposes of the product or performance and the intended audience

   b. Uses a range of information technology applications in creating the product or performance

   c. Incorporates principles of design and communication

   d. Communicates clearly and with a style that supports the purposes of the intended audience

STANDARD FIVE

The information literate student understands many of the economic, legal, and social issues surrounding the use of information and accesses and uses information ethically and legally.

Performance Indicators

1. The information literate student understands many of the ethical, legal, and socioeconomic issues surrounding information and information technology.

   Outcomes Include

   a. Identifies and discusses issues related to privacy and security in both the print and electronic environments

   b. Identifies and discusses issues related to free vs. fee-based access to information

   c. Identifies and discusses issues related to censorship and freedom of speech

   d. Demonstrates an understanding of intellectual property, copyright, and fair use of copyrighted material

2. The information literate student follows laws, regulations, institutional policies, and etiquette related to the access and use of information resources.

   Outcomes Include

   a. Participates in electronic discussions following accepted practices (e.g., netiquette)

b. Uses approved passwords and other forms of ID for access to information resources

c. Complies with institutional policies on access to information resources

d. Preserves the integrity of information resources, equipment, systems, and facilities

e. Legally obtains, stores, and disseminates text, data, images, or sounds

f. Demonstrates an understanding of what constitutes plagiarism and does not represent work attributable to others as his/her own

g. Demonstrates an understanding of institutional policies related to human subjects research

3. The information literate student acknowledges the use of information sources in communicating the product or performance.

Outcomes Include

a. Selects an appropriate documentation style and uses it consistently to cite sources

b. Posts permission granted notices, as needed, for copyrighted material

APPENDIX B DEFINING MOMENTS IN INFORMATION LITERACY

STARTING WITH THE FIRST RECOGNIZED use of the term *information literacy*, the following list highlights some of the key moments in the evolution of the understanding and interpretation of IL.

Pre-1980s	Technology was seen primarily as a tool to complete tasks, especially within the workplace
Post-1980s	Networked technologies enabled anyone to create, store, and access information anywhere in the world, thereby expanding perceptions about computer technologies
1974	Paul Zurkowski credited with coining the term *information literacy*
1976	Lee Burchinal among the first to link IL to emergent information technologies and networks
1979	Eugene Garfield expands definition beyond the workplace
1983	*A Nation at Risk* talks about information in education and the workplace in the knowledge society
	Microcomputer chosen as Machine of the Year by *Time* magazine, focusing attention on using computers to accomplish tasks and perform specific functions
	Forest Woody Horton discusses distinction between computer literacy and information literacy, laying the groundwork for modern definitions of information literacy

1986   William Demo discusses emergent communication technologies (e.g., e-mail) and the fact that information is no longer the sole province of libraries and librarians (i.e., information literacy is important beyond the library)

    Carnegie Foundation Report on Colleges is one of a growing number of publications discussing concerns about graduating students' ability to succeed in the new age

1987   "Libraries and the Search for Academic Excellence" symposium held to discuss the role of academic libraries in the reform movement, pushing IL to the forefront of general education agenda

1989   American Library Association's Presidential Committee on Information Literacy formed to define IL, design a model, and determine implications; provided list of requisite skills that have since become the foundation of most current understandings and definitions of IL

    National Forum on Information Literacy (NFIL) formed to identify trends in information literacy and to bring various groups together

    Information Literacy: Revolution in the Library published, talking about the role of librarians in the teaching and learning process (particularly with respect to information literacy) and observing that the education of information literate graduates was a joint responsibility to be shared by everyone—librarians, faculty, and administrators alike

1990   Secretary of Labor's Commission on Achieving Necessary Skills (SCANS) formed to study the skills that contemporary workers need to succeed; resultant report closely parallels the final report of ALA's Presidential Committee on Information Literacy

    Mike Eisenberg and Bob Berkowitz develop Big6 Skills Model, a process model of IL focusing on how people solve information problems

1992   Christina Doyle publishes the results of a Delphi study and expands the definition of IL based on responses from more than a hundred librarians and other information professionals noted for their work in or contributions to IL

1997   Christine Bruce publishes *The Seven Faces of Information Literacy*, which presents a relational model of IL acknowledging individual interpretations of what is meant by the term; her model not only articulates seven characterizations of IL but also examines how individuals relate to information itself

Pre-2000   Trend emerges of interpreting IL as an inclusive term that encompasses other literacies (e.g., business, computer, health)

2000 to present   ALA definition of IL evolves into a series of standards that are subsequently reviewed and approved by the ACRL board of directors on January 1, 2000

In 2002, Educational Testing Service convenes the International Information and Communication Technology (ICT) Literacy Panel to better understand and assess IL, to better understand how people think about information while using technology (especially when communicating information), and to try to address perceived shortcomings of existing IL models and definitions; articulates seven proficiencies and descriptions as part of its ICT literacy model

APPENDIX C OVERVIEW OF INSTRUCTION IN AMERICAN LIBRARIES

APPROACHES TO LIBRARY INSTRUCTION MAY be loosely grouped into five chronological categories: library orientation, library instruction, course integration, credit-bearing courses, and information literacy instruction. Most libraries and universities use at least one of those approaches when instructing students in the use of information.

LIBRARY ORIENTATION
Late 1800s

- Links between libraries and instruction began to emerge
- Stacks began to be open to students, resulting in the need to educate students about how to locate materials
- Instructional focus was on location of things (e.g., tours), books, and the creation of bibliographies
- At the first American Library Association conference (1876), Melvil Dewey linked libraries with schools, implied that librarians played a key part in the education process, and characterized librarians as essentially teachers
- Raymond C. Davis, a librarian from the University of Michigan, began giving lectures (1879) on the use of the card catalog and reference materials and was among the first to suggest a bibliography course to discuss the history of books and printing and how information was organized in a library

Early 1900s

- As the amount of information grew, tours and orientations were seen as insufficient; instruction about the entire library, not just about books, became necessary
- The first planned instruction took place at Columbia University (1909)
- William Warner Bishop (librarian, Princeton University) wrote that students from elementary school through college should be trained in how to use the library effectively (1912)

Pre–World War II

- Libraries were becoming more integrated into the curriculum and into the college setting as a whole
- Librarians were still primarily specialists

LIBRARY INSTRUCTION
Post–World War II

- Enrollments began to increase dramatically as the space race and other developments resulted in legislation and budgets more supportive of colleges and universities
- Librarians were evolving from specialists to generalists in order to better deal with the growing amount and variety of information
- Instruction became increasingly lecture based, and students were asked to complete assignments based on the lecture
- Because they tended to focus on the whole library and were task oriented, such presentations were often referred to as library instruction

COURSE INTEGRATION
1960s to 1970s

- Instruction began to be embedded into the entire curriculum
- Patricia Bryan Knapp (1966) called for replacing the one-shot library-orientation model with a program of instruction that developed competence over a period of time and focused on the organization of information, the identification of core works, and the importance of evaluating and interpreting information
- The Earlham College model, developed by Evan Farber, Thomas Kirk, and James Kennedy, emphasized faculty-librarian collaboration, assignment-based instruction, and the belief that working together was necessary to ensure the success of any instructional program involving the library
- In his 1964 article "Anachronistic Wizard: The College Reference Librarian" Daniel Gore was among the first to call for separate, librarian-taught courses and outlined a basic one-semester course that he felt could be taught by any librarian

CREDIT-BEARING COURSES
1970s to 1980s

- The growing importance of library instruction can be linked to a number of developments within the field of librarianship, such as

  - The creation of the ACRL's Bibliographic Instruction Task Force (1971), which in 1977 became the Bibliographic Instruction Section

  - The start of Project LOEX (Library Orientation and Instruction Exchange; 1972) as a means for librarians to stay abreast of developments in instruction

  - ALA's creation of the Library Instruction Round Table (1977)

- As students became more self-directed and basic library orientation was increasingly seen as inadequate, instruction evolved from a task-oriented approach to one that was more process driven
- Although focusing instruction on a specific assignment or course was important, it did not allow the depth desired or often needed by students; in response, credit-bearing courses were suggested as a solution

INFORMATION LITERACY INSTRUCTION
1990s and beyond

- The notion that information literacy instruction needed to be embedded throughout the curriculum rather than limited to the library or specific courses or disciplines began to become more commonplace
- Growing emphasis was placed on the process of information seeking rather than on specific resources (e.g., bibliographic instruction) or library-specific skills (e.g., library orientation)
- Process models recognize that information exists at all levels of society and that individuals need a variety of skills to effectively navigate the ever-growing sea of information
- In 1994, San Jose State University was among the first to develop a campuswide information literacy program—the Information Literacy Initiative
- Patricia Breivik's 1998 book *Student Learning in the Information Age* was among the first to advocate course-integrated instruction involving extensive faculty-librarian collaboration in all courses across the entire curriculum for all students
- Publications such as "Information Literacy Competency Standards for Higher Education" (2000) and "Objectives for Information Literacy Instruction: A Model Statement for Academic Librarians" (2001) were among the first to provide academic librarians and faculty members with the tools to work collaboratively to incorporate information literacy into the curriculum

- Carol C. Kuhlthau (1991) was among the first to conduct empirical studies of how people seek information and is often associated with the shift to thinking of information literacy as a user-driven process rather than a resource-driven one
- Developed in 1990 by Michael Eisenberg and Bob Berkowitz, the Big6 Skills Model looks at any need for information as a problem to be solved, whether for homework or for situations outside the classroom

REFERENCES

American Library Association. Presidential Committee on Information Literacy. 1989. Final Report. Chicago: ALA. Available online at www.ala.org/ala/mgrps/divs/acrl/publications/whitepapers/presidential.cfm.

Association of College and Research Libraries. 2000. "Information Literacy Competency Standards for Higher Education." Chicago: ALA. Available online at www.ala.org/ala/mgrps/divs/acrl/standards/informationliteracycompetency.cfm.

Behrens, Shirley J. 1994. "A Conceptual Analysis and Historical Overview of Information Literacy." *College and Research Libraries* 55 (4): 309–322.

Boekhorst, A. K., and J. J. Britz. 2004. "Information Literacy at School Level: A Comparative Study between the Netherlands and South Africa." *South African Journal of Library and Information Science* 70 (2): 63–71.

Breivik, Patricia Senn. 2005. "21st Century Learning and Information Literacy." *Change* 37 (2): 20–27.

Dolence, Michael G., and Donald M. Norris. 1995. "Transforming Higher Education: A Vision for Learning in the 21st Century." Ann Arbor, MI: Society for College and University Planning.

Doyle, Christina S. 1994. "Information Literacy in an Information Society: A Concept for the Information Age." Washington, DC: ERIC Clearinghouse on Information and Technology (ERIC Document Reproduction Service No. ED 372763).

Grassian, E. S., and J. R. Kaplowitz. 2001. *Information Literacy Instruction: Theory and Practice*. New York: Neal-Schuman.

Gumport, Patricia J., and Marc Chun. 2005. "Technology and Higher Education: Opportunities and Challenges for the New Era." In *American Higher Education in the 21st Century: Societal, Political, and Economic Challenges,* ed. Philip G. Altbach, Robert O. Berdahl, and Patricia J. Gumport. 2nd ed. Baltimore: Johns Hopkins University Press.

Joyce, C. Alan, ed. 2007. *The World Almanac and Book of Facts 2008.* New York: World Almanac Education Group.

McCrank, L. J. 1992. "Academic Programs for Information Literacy: Theory and Structure." *RQ* 31: 485–497.

Salony, Mary F. 1995. "The History of Bibliographic Instruction: Changing Trends from Books to the Electronic World." *Reference Librarian,* no. 51–52: 31–51.

Thompson, Gary B. 2002. "Information Literacy Accreditation Mandates: What They Mean for Faculty and Librarians." *Library Trends* 51 (2): 218–241.

INDEX

Note: Page numbers followed by *t* or *f* indicate tables or figures, respectively.

A

academic freedom
  as defense for bad assignments, 27
  and resistance to change, 21
access procedures, changes in, 49
accreditation standards and information
      literacy, 5
ACRL. *See* Association of College and
      Research Libraries (ACRL) standards
administrative issues and failed assignments,
      36–39
alternate versions or editions, acceptability
      of, 106–107
anticipation of needs, 130–131
APA (American Psychological Association)
      citation style, 80, 81–82t, 107
approachability of librarians
  and collaboration with faculty, 22
  and relations with students, 125–126
assessment. *See* evaluation of assignments
assigned topics, difficulties with, 63–65, 70
assignment awareness, 19t
assignment notebook, 130
assignment transactions, 14–18
  dynamics of, 16–18
  life cycle of, 14–16
assignments
  challenges to assisting students, 125–128
  as focus of classroom instruction time,
      120, 122

interpretation of by librarian, 129
librarians' exclusion from development
      of, 15–16
linked to scavenger hunts, 106
role of IL in, 4–5, 7–10
See also essay assignments; scavenger
      hunts; term papers; tours
assignments, failure of
  librarians' response to, 28–29
  reasons for, 33–36
assignments, problematic, 23–28
  feedback on, 17, 24, 25t, 27, 34, 130
  handling frustration at, 133–134
  librarian-faculty relationships in, 27–
      28
  methods of contact, 24–25, 26t
  triage of, 26–27
  unclear purpose, 34–35, 104–105
  unclear requirements, 126
  unclear terminology, 34–35, 61–65
Association of College and Research
      Libraries (ACRL) standards, 10, 46,
      135–142

B

backup files, failure to create, 37–38
birth date assignments, drawbacks of, 58–
      59
browser buttons, misuse of, 43
browsing and meta-searching, 52–53

C

change, resistance to, 21, 47–49

changes to resources and failed assignments, 36

Chicago Manual of Style (CMS) citation style, 80, 81–82t

citation management software, 45, 79

citation of sources, 75–82

   citation styles, 79–82

   expectations of in creation of assignments, 10

   inaccurate citations in assignments, 36–37

   students' difficulties with, 76–79

classroom instruction, 117–124

   benefits, 118

   dos and don'ts, 123

   evaluation of session, 119–120

   faculty resentment of time required for, 14, 20

   limited content in, 120–121

   planning of session, 118–119

   preparation time for, 121–122

   See also one-shot workshops

CMS (*Chicago Manual of Style*) citation style, 80, 81–82t

collaboration with faculty, 13–28

   barriers to, 13–14

   challenges in, 18–21

   development of, 21–23

   feedback on problematic assignments, 23–28

   See also faculty-librarian relationships; feedback on assignments; meetings with faculty

committees, librarian's service on, 22

compatibility between hardware and software, 53

computer configurations and updates, 85

computer skills

   vs. research skills, 43–44

   students' lack of, 121

connectivity issues, 49

content-oriented assignments, 68, 69–70

course integration of library instruction, history of, 148

credit-bearing courses in library instruction, history of, 149

curriculum, difficulties of incorporating IL into, 6t, 20–21

curriculum development, librarian's participation in, 23

D

databases

   search strategies for, 52

   unclear meaning of term, 61

dial-up access to Internet, 49, 85

disabled students, communications with, 110, 126

downloading software. *See* software downloads

E

electronic resources

   changes in, 47–49

   limited access to, 35–36

   limited availability of, 41–42

   navigation of, 43

   restrictions on use of in assignments, 57–58

   in scavenger hunts, 106

   skills required to access, 44

   unclear meaning of term, 61

   See also resources

encyclopedias, limitations on use of, 69–70

equipment-related issues, 53, 59

essay assignments

   definition, 55–56

   problems, 60–61

   types of, 62t

   See also writing-from-sources and essay assignments

ethics

   in IL standards, 5

   and requiring citation of sources, 76

evaluation of assignments, 9, 15–16

   in creation of assignments, 7–8

evaluation of library instruction, 119–120

evaluation of resources, skills in, 43–44

examples in classroom instruction, 122

expectations

   in creation of assignments, 7–8, 10

   overly optimistic, 69

   on use of citations, 78

extra-credit assignments, scavenger hunts as, 104, 110

F

faculty, problems for librarians
 criticism of faculty by librarians, 96
 failure to check use of citations, 78
 as information literacy instructors, 20
 preference for assigned topics, 64
 resistance to change, 21
 use of scavenger hunts to increase
  personal knowledge of library, 112
faculty orientation, 23
 for changes in resources, 48
 for new resources and services, 112
 for new technology, 54
 See also professional development for
  faculty
faculty-librarian relationships, 18, 20–21
 and classroom instruction, 123
 development of, 21–23
 and feedback on problematic
  assignments, 17, 24, 25t, 27, 34, 130
 role of librarian misunderstood by
  faculty, 18
 strategies for, 133–134
 See also collaboration with faculty;
  meetings with faculty
faculty-student relationships, 17
failure, coping with, 133
feedback on assignments
 contacting faculty for, 24, 25t
 librarians as means of providing, 17
 unclear assignments, 27, 34
files, inaccessible, and failure of
  assignments, 37–38
firewalls and access to online resources, 84
frustration, coping with, 133

G

grading criteria
 scavenger hunts, 104
 use of citations, 78

H

handouts in classroom instruction, 121
hands-on activities, advantages and
  disadvantages, 120
hardware, skills for, 53. *See also* equipment-
  related issues
hardware and software incompatibility, 53
help services for remote users, 87–89

HTML text, restrictions on use of, 70
hybrid IL instruction, definition, 7

I

IL instruction. *See* information literacy
  instruction
inaccurate information in library guides and
  tours, 96, 97
inappropriate resources, use of, 51
inappropriate search terms, 51–52
indexes, printed, use of, 58, 96
information literacy
 definition, 3–4
 history, 5, 143–145
information literacy instruction
 in continuum of instruction in the
  library, 118
 history, 149–150
 models of, 7, 8t
information technology, definition, 45–46.
  See also technology
institutional governance as hindrance to
  collaboration, 20
integrated IL instruction, definition, 7
interlibrary loan as requirement in
  assignments, 71–72, 112
international students, communications
  with, 110, 126
Internet websites
 vs. databases, 52, 54
 dial-up access to, 49, 85
 limitations on use of, 69–70
 quality of information on, 44, 54
irrelevant assignments, scavenger hunts as,
  104

K

knowledge economy and effective
  assignments, 4–5

L

legal issues in IL standards, 5
liaison, librarians assigned as
 and awareness of assignments, 129
 effectiveness of, 21–22
librarian mediation required for resource
  access, 41, 85
librarian-assignment dynamic, 18, 128–
  129

librarian-faculty relationships. *See* faculty-
    librarian relationships
librarians, communication among
    about problematic assignments, 24, 34
    and misperception that librarians have
        all the answers, 42
    sharing information about assignments,
        122–123, 130
    See also staff, burdens on
librarian-student relationships
    in classroom instruction, 122
    dos and don'ts, 131
    dynamics of, 17–18
    in library, 125–126
    misperception that librarians have all the
        answers, 42
    in scavenger hunts, 110–111
library as place
    and scavenger hunts, 102, 104
    and tours, 95, 98
    variations in arrangement of, 43
library guides, disadvantages, 95–96
library instruction
    definition, 5–7
    history, 148
    See also classroom instruction;
        information literacy instruction; one-
        shot workshops
library orientation, 118, 147–148
library resources and services, requiring use
    of, 57, 112
library websites, changes in, 47
licensing restrictions and remote access,
    49–50, 85–86
limited availability of printed resources,
    57–58, 106
listening to students, 129–130
location of resources, changes in, 47

M
meetings with faculty
    and anticipation of needs, 131
    attendance of librarians at faculty
        meetings, 22
    disadvantages of, 20
    on problematic assignments, 26, 130
meta-searching, 52–53
microfilm collections, use of, 58–59, 103

MLA (Modern Language Association)
    citation style, 80, 81–82t

N
name changes in resources, 47
navigation of electronic resources, 43
needs assessment of students for classroom
    instruction, 121
nonintegrated IL instruction, 7
nonproductive activities, requiring, 71

O
one-shot workshops
    insufficiency of, 40–41
    role in IL instruction, 6, 65
    sample format for, 124
    on use of citation management software,
        79
    See also classroom instruction
"online," ambiguous meaning of, 35, 44
online research in assignments, 83–89
organizational structure of library and
    scavenger hunts, 104
organizing ideas in writing-from-sources
    assignments, 56
outcomes in creation of assignments, 7, 10
outdated resources in assignments, 73

P
paraphrased material and citation of
    sources, 76–77
passwords and difficulty accessing resources,
    41–42, 84
peer-reviewed resources
    appropriateness of, 60–61
    searching for, 48, 49
    students' difficulty in understanding, 69
perceived value of scavenger hunt items,
    108–109
personal bibliographic software. *See* citation
    management software
perspective, topics lacking a specific, 63
plagiarism
    and assigned topics, 64, 65
    by remote users, 89
    students' lack of awareness of
        consequences of, 78
plagiarism-detecting software, 79, 89

plug-ins on library website, 86
pop-up blocking and access to online
        resources, 84
printed resources
    assignments intended to teach value of,
        57–58
    indexes, 58, 96
    unavailability of, 106
printing, costs of, 38–39
process-oriented assignments, 9
procrastination, 128
product-oriented assignments, 9, 34
professional development for faculty, 22–23.
        See also faculty orientation
promotion of library resources, 48–49
purpose of assignment, 34–35, 104–105.
        See also outcomes in creation of
        assignments

Q

quoted material, citation of, 76–77

R

reference books, assignments using, 72
reference interview. *See* students, working
        with
reference management software. *See*
        citation management software
relevance of resource in assignments
    microfilm collections, 59, 103
    tours, 98–99
remote access
    challenges of assignments using, 83–84
    communications with users, 87–89
    difficulties in, 49–50
    effect on traditional measures of library
        use, 14
    and monitoring for plagiarism, 89
    technology of in classroom instruction,
        121
    and tours, 98
requirements
    students unclear on, 126
    for term/research papers, 67–68
research papers vs. term papers, 67. *See also*
        term papers
research process
    and scavenger hunts, 109–110

students' lack of experience with, 72–
        73
    in writing-from-sources assignments, 56
research skills
    misperception of students' skills, 39–40
    research as difficult, 42, 105–106
    students' lack of basic library skills, 65
research topics. *See* topic development;
        topic selection
research-focused assignments
    common problems, 70–72
    term papers, 68
resource availability
    changes in resources or access methods,
        36, 49
    in creation of assignments, 9, 64
    missing from library, 35–36, 73
    to remote users, 85–86
    in scavenger hunts, 106–107
resource relevance. *See* relevance of
        resource in assignments
resources
    changes in interface, 48–49
    identification of appropriate, 51
    See also electronic resources; printed
        resources
retrieval skills in creation of assignments, 9
reverse scavenger hunts, 102

S

scavenger hunts, 101–114
    dos and don'ts, 113–114
    items for, 105
    purposes, 102
    as tours, 103, 109
    what not to do, 102–104
scholarly publication and citation of
        sources, 76
scripts for tours, 97
search strategies
    difficulties in generating, 126–127
    problems with, 50–53
    spelling in, 52, 73
security applications and access to online
        resources, 37, 84
signatures of staff in scavenger hunts, 111
software downloads
    from library website, 86

software downloads (cont.)
   security restrictions on, 37, 41–42, 84
   and time-out features in resources, 49
software for downloading and formatting
      citations, 45, 79
software problems
   security limitations on library computers,
      37, 84
   students' lack of skills for using, 53
   use of incompatible versions, 38, 86
source material, use of, 76–77
special collections, limited availability of,
      41–42
special needs students, communications
      with, 110, 126
spelling
   in citation management software, 79
   in search strategies, 52, 73
staff, burdens on
   filling bogus ILL requests, 71–72
   help with microfilm machines, 59
   as object of scavenger hunts, 103
   scavenger hunts, 107, 108, 110–111, 112
standards for information literacy, 3–4
student-librarian relationships. See librarian-
      student relationships
students
   lack of computer skills, 121
   lack of experience in research process,
      72–73
   misperception that they don't need help,
      43
   perceptions of library shaped by faculty,
      14
   relations with faculty, 17
   relations with librarians, 17–18
   unclear on requirements for assignment,
      126
students, working with, 125–131
students' lack of experience
   in citing sources, 76–79
   in research process, 39–40, 121
   using resources and course materials
      off-site, 84
substitutions for resources, acceptability of,
      73
suggested topics, difficulties with, 63–65, 70

summarized material, citation of, 76–77
support for remote users, levels of, 88–89
synonyms and alternative terms as search
      terms, 51. See also search strategies

T

technology
   barriers to completion of assignments,
      37–39
   in classroom instruction, 121
   and computer configurations, 85
   response to changes in, 47–49
   and security limitations on library
      computers, 37, 84
   skills required for use of, 46
   unavailability of, 53–54
   use of incompatible technologies, 38
   See also information technology
term papers
   common problems, 69–72
   dos and don'ts, 74
   vs. research papers, 67
terminology, unclear. See assignments,
      problematic
term-paper factories, 79
time frame
   formatting citations, 75
   and procrastinating students, 128
   scavenger hunts, 101
   term papers or research papers, 68
   tours, 93
   writing-from-sources and essay
      assignments, 56
time-out features in electronic resources, 49
topic development
   helping students with, 50–51, 63, 73
   sample assignment, 72
topic selection
   difficulties in, 62–63, 127–128
   and meta-searching, 52–53
   topics not supported by adequate
      resources, 63
   in writing-from-sources assignments, 56
tours, 93–100
   dos and don'ts, 100
   by faculty, 96–97
   logistics, 98

selection of material for, 97
types of, 94t
what not to do, 95–96

U

unclear terminology in assignments. *See*
    assignments, problematic
unfamiliarity with academic libraries, 65
users, limits on number of, 50

V

virtual tours, 95, 98, 99

W

websites. *See* Internet websites; library
    websites
workshops. *See* one-shot workshops
writing-from-sources and essay assignments
    dos and don'ts, 66
    issues, 61–65
    problems, 57–61, 65
    purposes of, 56–57
    See also essay assignments

You may also be interested in

Marketing Today's Academic Library: Brian Mathews uses his vast experience to propose new visions and ideas for matching services with student needs, challenging the traditional way of thinking and providing a framework to target users more precisely.

Creating the Customer-Driven Academic Library: Librarians are now faced with marketing to a generation of students who log on rather than walk in. This cutting-edge book supplies the tools needed to keep customers coming through the door.

Protecting Intellectual Freedom in Your Academic Library: This title presents a number of scenarios in which intellectual freedom is at risk and includes case studies that provide narrative treatment of common situations tailored to academic libraries, with sidebars throughout that offer sample policies, definitions of key terms, and analysis of important statutes and decisions.

Teaching Information Literacy, Second Edition: Covering the basics of planning research and collecting and evaluating sources, these 50 lessons show how to engage with electronic and print information resources alike, and they can be used as a full semester course or as a single focused seminar or workshop.

Order today at www.alastore.ala.org or 866-746-7252!